HOOYAH!

UDT/SEAL STORIES OF THE 1960'S

SECOND EDITION

RICHARD G. "NICK" NICKELSON

HERITAGE BOOKS
2022

HERITAGE BOOKS
AN IMPRINT OF HERITAGE BOOKS, INC.

Books, CDs, and more—Worldwide

For our listing of thousands of titles see our website
at
www.HeritageBooks.com

Published 2022 by
HERITAGE BOOKS, INC.
Publishing Division
5810 Ruatan Street
Berwyn Heights, MD 20740

Copyright © 2006 Richard G. "Nick" Nickelson

All rights reserved. No part of this book may be reproduced or transmitted in any form or by any means, electronic or mechanical, including photocopying, recording or by any information storage and retrieval system without written permission from the author, except for the inclusion of brief quotations in a review.

International Standard Book Number
Paperbound: 978-0-7884-4250-6

Routine and offbeat exploits
that team members have been
talking and laughing about
for years.

Some are humorous
and
some are not.

CONTENTS

INTRODUCTION
GRADUATION – CLASS # 28
BEFORE TRAINING:
   1.   THE TEAMS OVERSEAS
   2.   TO TRAINING

HELL WEEK:
   3.   GOOD ADVICE
   4.   TWO NIGHTS IN HELL WEEK
   5.   NIGHT PROBLEMS
   6.   LAST MAN STANDING
   7.   CHECKING IN
   8.   A FREE RIDE
   9.   MUTE SCREAMS AND JELLY BEANS

POST HELL WEEK TRAINING:
  10.   DO YOU WANT TO QUIT?
  11.   COLD TESTED
  12.   YOU ARE WHAT YOU EAT
  13.   CLASS-28 VS. MARINES
  14.   LACK OF SLEEP AND BOOBY-TRAPS
  15.   BLOWING THINGS UP
  16.   A CRITICAL SITUATION
  17.   THE SWIM THAT DIDN'T HAPPEN

GOOD TIMES IN THE TEAMS:
  18.   THE OLD OAK TREE
  19.   TESTING NEW EQUIPMENT
  20.   HOOYAH! THE WORD
  21.   GARY LANPHIER AND THE DEVIL CAR
  22.   TO SEE OR NOT TO SEA
  23.   THAT WAS NO FERRY BOAT RIDE
  24.   1962 AND THE CUBAN MISSILE CRISES
  25.   BODY SEARCH PANAMA
  26.   ICE CREAM AND STRAWBERIES

27.	BEARTRACKS AND THE PILOT
28.	TRIUMPH MOTOR CYCLES
29.	THE SILVER STRAND
30.	FASTER WASN'T NECESSARLY BETTER
31.	FRIENDSHIP CAME LATER
32.	PROJECT MERCURY: FAITH 7
33.	JUMP SCHOOL
34.	A NIGHT IN NOVEMBER
35.	FROM UDT TO SEAL
36.	THE STANDING FISHERMAN
37.	A TIME OF REFLECTION
38.	BODY SEARCH AND RECOVERY
39.	RIP TIDE
40.	LEO HAMEL – MASTER CHIEF
41.	JOHNSTON ISLAND
42.	NAVAL PENTATHLON
43.	LEAVING THE TEAMS

INTRODUCTION

The 1960's, ten years filled with untold challenges for those hearty enough to have been inducted into the ranks of Naval Special Warfare. Through the mid 1960's, the combined strength of the U.S. Navy's four Underwater Demolition Teams (UDT), plus two Sea Air Land (SEAL) Units, numbered fewer than five hundred men. Though small in number, this cadre of men would become an integral part in what would be one of the most demanding and exciting periods in American history.

The race against Russia to be the first in space and on the moon, the Cuban Missile Crisis, and Vietnam were but three challenges facing Naval Special Warfare. In addition, there would be the assimilation of new and untested diving equipment, previously untried swimmer recovery systems, high-speed boats propelled by turbo-jet engines, plus both high and low altitude parachuting. Yes, during the early to mid 1960's, all of the above would be integrated into the everyday life of those men serving in Naval Special Warfare Units more commonly known as "The Teams."

For this particular period of time, much has been written about UDT/SEAL Team involvement in Vietnam, while little has been documented relevant to the routine and offbeat exploits Team members have been talking and laughing about for years. Therefore, the primary objective of this book is to record known, but previously undocumented events that occurred in the Teams. In part, these stories relate to the *Mercury* Space Program, Cuban Missile Crisis, Team training problems, Naval Pentathlon, plus routine daily activities that made up the lives of these men. Some stories are humorous and others are not.

A secondary objective of this book is to record what happened during memorable training exercises, with emphasis on the lighter side of Basic Underwater

Demolition SEAL Training (BUDS). This book is, therefore, intended to tell stories, most of which I witnessed first-hand or was a party to. In addition, incidents are being documented that have been passed on to me. Though they are based on secondhand information, other Team members have verified their validity. It is also my intention to deal with some of the more memorable moments of BUDS, as experienced by members of West Coast Class-28, my class.

Each of the stories related to Hell Week occurred over a relatively short time frame, usually no more than several hours. While Hell Week lasted for seven days, or one hundred sixty-eight hours, the stories in this book cover no more than fifteen to twenty of those hours. Each story is true, as are the individuals mentioned in them. Sadly, the names mentioned are few because the majority of the stories deal with the boat crew to which I was assigned. Therefore, these stories encompass only a small portion of Hell Week, which happened more than forty years ago, during the first of two classes conducted on the West Coast in 1962.

It would have been inappropriate not to incorporate stories that occurred during post Hell Week, BUDS, training. Therefore, those that have been included relate to individuals that I was close to during training but, in several instances, these stories relate to the entire class. There are many more stories that could have been written and certainly deserve mention. Many more are unknown to me or have been forgotten. If I excluded anyone, I apologize because every man that completed BUDS and graduated as a member of Class-28 is deserving of mention.

Some of the stories shared with you here relate to specific events and are intended to show a little of what life was like in the Teams. Others are humorous and depict the style or character of the individual capable of succeeding in the Teams. All stories, however, were written with the deepest respect for the individual who made that story possible.

UNDERWATER DEMOLITION TRAINING DIVISION
NAVAL AMPHIBIOUS SCHOOL
CORONADO, CALIFORNIA

GRADUATION CLASS #28
27 JULY 1962

INSTRUCTORS

LT J.W. SUDDUTH
LT J.M. STEPHENSON
LT L.C. SCHMIDT
LT J.B. BATTON

BRERETON, R.G., QMC-P1
PRICE, A.S., ENCA
MURPHY, K.R., ENCA

ALLEN, R., BM1-P1
CIFUENTES, C.L., BM1
JURIC, F.J., RD1-P1
DICKERSON, R.L., EM1-P1
HARMAN, G.K., YN1
FILLMORE, J.A., EN2
BARBER, J.P., HM2

GRADUATION CLASS

LTJG W.R. EDDINS
LTJG A.N. GRISEMER
LTJG M.F. PAUL
LTJG P.E. RIDDLE
ENS R.E. BRIGHT
ENS C.E. CARNEY
ENS L.G. DEL MUNDO
ENS T.O. DUNNE
ENS J.E. FOX
ENS D.L. MANN

ANDERSON, W.W., EON2
BAKER, W.J., SA
BODKIN, D.M., SA
BOURKARD, R.R., SA
BRANNON, A.W., SA
CHICKVARY, J.A., SA
COPELAND, F.T., SA
DOWD, T.C., SA
DOYLE, W.T., SA
FARIS, R.A., SA
FLETCHER, A.L., SN
FOLEY, J.D., SN

FORD, W.L., SA
FREEMAN, G.M., SA
HALE, A.R., EON2
HANCOCK, R.L., AN
LABRESH, R.L., SA
LANPHIER, G.L., PR3
MAC MASTER, J.R., SA
MILLER, L.E., RM3
MILLS, W.H., SA
NICKELSON, R.G., DM3
OLSON, R.D., SA
PATE, J.E., SM2
PHELPS, G.A., SA
SMITH, D.F., SA
STANSELL, J.H., SA
STILLWELL, A.G., SA
SWAGEMAKERS, A.A., SA
SWEPSTON, C.E., GM2
TUSI, R.L., HM2
WAGNER, R.K., SK2
WALSH, C.L., SA
WRIGHT, W.F., SM3
ZIMOS, A.G., SA

GRADUATION CLASS # 28
27 JULY 1962

At the beginning of training, the question most often asked was "Who of those trainees assigned to Class-28 will complete the Basic Underwater Demolition SEAL Training?" On this day, that question had been answered. These 45 graduates, from the first of two West Coast BUDS Training Classes conducted during 1962, had successfully completed the program and were accepted into the realms of "Navy Frogmen." These men would now take their places in UDT-11 and UDT-12, with one graduate being assigned to SEAL Team One.

BEFORE TRAINING:

1. THE TEAMS OVERSEAS

While in the Continental United States, all West Coast UDT/SEAL Teams call the Coronado Naval Amphibious Base home. The Team Compound is situated on the Silver Strand, just south of Coronado. In addition, it is customary to station a UDT/SEAL Detachment at a base in the Far East. This has been the standard mode of operation since the conclusion of World War II. The overseas detachment performs various duties related to diving and demolitions but is there primarily as a show of force and to support Far East Operations.

In 1961, the Team's Far East Headquarters was Yokosuka, Japan. This is a large Naval Base that served as homeport for a number of U.S. Naval ships including the U.S.S. *Saint Paul*. The *Saint Paul* is a heavy cruiser that served as Flag Ship for the Commander of the 7th Fleet. The Yokosuka Naval Base was constructed at the conclusion of World War II to serve the U.S. Navy's COMWESPAC during the occupation of Japan by American Forces. A Garrison of Marines was assigned to provide security for the base, and their duties included overseeing the base brig and serving as sentries at all base entrances, as well as other duties performed by Marines.

As the story goes, sometime during 1961, members of the UDT Detachment assigned to this Naval Station had words with the Marines who manned the main entrance to the Naval Base. This wasn't unusual because UDT and Marine personnel have a long history of bumping heads. Marines claim that during war, when a beachhead has to be assaulted, they are the first ashore. You know: "The few, the proud, the Marines." On the other hand, men in the Teams claim, and rightly so, that Marines only go ashore after UDT/SEAL Teams have first cleared the beaches of all obstacles and hazards, thereby making it safe for them to do so. Anyway, I think you get the picture.

Over the next several weeks, animosity between Team members and the Marines grew until it came to an eventual head. Things finally boiled over when members of the UDT Detachment, returning from a diving operation, were refused access to the base by Marine sentries manning the main gate. Words were exchanged, a fight ensued, and the Marines lost. At this point, two of the Marine sentries were led to a flagpole, just inside the main gate, forced to face each other on opposite sides of the flagpole, and then handcuffed together with their own handcuffs. There would be no way for the Marines to free themselves, unless they were strong enough to pull the flagpole from the ground, and they weren't. The other Marine sentries who had been involved in the altercation were then tied up and placed in the back room of their guardhouse, which was located near the main entrance to the base. At this point, the men from the UDT Detachment simply yawned, climbed back into their truck, and then drove onto the base, leaving the main gate unattended.

You can imagine the scorn and disapproval this brought from the Base Commanding Officer (C.O.), not to mention the shame this incident levied on the Marine Garrison stationed at Yokosuka. It seemed that the only way to bring closure to this situation would be by punishing the responsible UDT members; after all, the Marines couldn't have been at fault. Though unlikely, had the men from the UDT Detachment lost, the matter would have been overlooked, and the Marines would have claimed bragging rights. This wasn't the case, however. Then, when the Officer in Charge of the UDT detachment refused to punish his men, the Base C.O. decided that the only real way to resolve this matter would be by expelling the entire UDT Detachment from his Naval

Base. He then called in the Officer in Charge and informed him that UDT was no longer welcome at the Yokosuka Naval Station and they were to leave immediately. Kind of like in the old cowboy movies, when the sheriff tells the villains they are to get out of Dodge before sunset.

When word of what had happened reached Coronado, the Commanding Officer of the Teams was upset, but in the Teams, things like this happen and are most often overlooked. It would have been a far bigger problem had his men lost to the Marines, but they hadn't and after all, it wasn't the end of the world. Next came a reprimand from Coronado's front office, then the UDT Detachment packed up their belongings, and the new Far East Headquarters, for all future UDT/SEAL Detachments, became Subic Bay, the Philippines.

When I entered the Navy in 1961, my first duty station was Yokosuka, Japan, aboard the U.S.S. *Saint Paul*. My plans had not included a shipboard duty assignment; this was not the reason I had joined the Navy. Life aboard a ship did not match the dream I had pursued since I was a young boy so therefore, I was not happy. However, I did what I had to do. I would serve one year aboard the *Saint Paul* before taking my first step toward becoming a member of one of the Navy's Special Operations Units.

I was seven years old when I first heard about the Navy's Underwater Demolition Units and what they did during the war. It was at that moment in my young life that I became hooked on becoming a Navy Frogman. My Father had served in the Navy during World War II and had returned home with many pictures and stories related to his service in the Pacific. A book of pictures depicting the numerous battles of the Pacific Theatre fascinated me. In that book, there was one picture that captivated my imagination; it was of a Navy Frogman. This picture wasn't of a man adorned in full diving gear with a knife between his teeth. No, it was simply a black and white photograph of a huge man, clad in a pair of khaki swim trunks. He had a long handlebar mustache and wore a smile that matched his size. He was standing in front of a boulder the size of a house and the caption under the picture read, "Naked Warrior." The picture was simple enough, but the impact it had on my young mind was far from simple. Yes, this is what I would be when I grew up. I convinced my dad to cut the picture from the book, and I then tacked it to the wall in my room. From that day, until the day I left home on active duty, that picture served as the basis for my inspiration. When I worked out or when things got tough at home or at school, the picture was there to inspire and give me hope.

During 1961, the year that I served on the *Saint Paul*, I saw little of the men who belonged to the UDT Detachment. They stayed pretty much to themselves and had little to do with "black shoes," a name given to those who served in the regular Navy. However, they did something for me that would prove invaluable when I applied for Basic Underwater Demolition SEAL Training (BUDS). They administered a swim test, one of the conditions for acceptance to training. Actually, there were five tests that had to be successfully completed by anyone desiring to attend BUDS. First, each candidate must pass a psychological examination conducted by a Navy Psychiatrist. Second, you must be able to withstand decompression in a chamber to a level of one hundred and twenty feet. Third, you must pass a swim test, conducted by someone from the Teams. Fourth, if under eighteen years old, you are required to provide a letter of consent, signed by your parents, holding the Navy faultless should something happen to you during training. Then fifth and the most difficult, at least in my case, approval from the duty command to which you are currently assigned.

I satisfactorily fulfilled the first four requirements and started to apply for BUDS. Disapproval was matched by disapproval until my fifth request when I was finally ordered to report to the Captain's quarters. For this request, I had added a new component: I would extend my enlistment two years if allowed to go to BUDS. I think it was this agreement that caught the Captain's attention, but at least he had agreed to talk to me. When I reported to his quarters, he asked why I was so insistent on going to the Teams. I explained my reasons, and he then said, "If you want me to approve this request, drop down and give me fifty push-ups." I did as the Captain ordered and when I recovered, or stood up, I asked him if he wanted fifty more. He laughed and said that wouldn't be necessary and then signed-off on my request. With that, I left the Captain's office, the U.S.S. *Saint Paul*, and on my eighteenth birthday, I said goodbye to Japan. As we flew from Japan to the United States, we crossed the International Dateline, and this provided a birthday that lasted two days. But the best was yet to come; I was on my way to BUDS and an introduction to what would prove to be the best and most rewarding years of my life.

2. TO TRAINING

Leaving Japan to attend Basic Underwater Demolition SEAL Training (BUDS) was one of the most exhilarating and satisfying moments of my life. After a year of applying for BUDS training, I had finally been accepted, making this also one of the happiest days of my life. Now, in order to get back to the Continental United States, I would hopefully take a flight from Japan. In the early nineteen sixties, a flight of this magnitude would require two days in the air, with stops at Midway Island and Guam. The alternative method of travel would have been riding the gray ghost, or a Navy ship, and that would have required nearly a month at sea, a prospect I dreaded thinking about.

I thanked God that a ship ride home wasn't in the equation, as I boarded the plane early on the twentieth of January, my eighteenth birthday. There couldn't have been a better birthday present than flying home, and I was ecstatic. I didn't talk to anyone on the plane about this fact, but as an extra bonus, this birthday would span two days. I didn't find out about this added day until our MATS pilot informed all of the passengers that we would see the sun rise and set twice on the twentieth. This would happen because we were to cross the International Date Line, thus requiring us to move our watches back a day. This was something special to share, but I decided to keep this fact to myself.

We arrived in San Francisco in the early afternoon, and I immediately caught a bus to the San Francisco International Airport. From there, I would catch another flight to Colorado Springs, my hometown before joining the Navy. It had snowed in San Francisco, a very rare occurrence, and the locals were going crazy. Cars were spinning out of control, and those not involved in an accident with another car were off the freeway in a ditch. No one seemed to mind; however, they appeared to be mesmerized by the unusual sight of this white substance called snow. Here I was, given a birthday that lasted two days and witnessing snow in San Francisco. This was quite a way to start my new life and to me, it certainly seemed like a good omen.

    I would now spend thirty days on leave in Colorado before I had to report to Coronado and training. This was one of those magical times that happen in everyone's life, but only rarely. All of the circumstances surrounding this transfer seemed to have some special significance. I am thankful that I can look back and realize how special that time in my life actually was. I had missed Colorado, my parents and friends, but was more excited about going to BUDS than anything else, and the month that I spent on leave went by slowly. When it finally came time to start the trip to Coronado, my parents felt it would be good if we drove together so they could see my new home. Also, Rita, my mother's sister lived in Los Angeles, so this would give my mother an opportunity to spend some quality time with her sister and niece Linda. Rita and Linda would serve as my extended family, the entire time I was in the Navy, and I will always be grateful for the love they shared with me.

    I loved California from the moment we arrived. As we were driving along the freeways of Los Angeles, I marveled at the beautiful palm trees that seemed to be everywhere, stretching their palm branches up toward heaven. Here it was February, and there were green lawns, flowers, sunshine, and warm days. We had left a very cold Colorado only a few days earlier, and now we were in the land of sunshine and sandy beaches; how could things ever get any better than this? There wasn't a doubt in my mind; we were where I belonged, where I wanted to be. And, though I didn't know it at the time, this is where I would spend the next forty-plus years of my life.

We arrived in San Diego late at night, so my parents decided it would be best to wait until the following morning before taking the ferryboat to Coronado. In the early sixties, there was no Coronado Bay Bridge. The only way to reach Coronado was the ferry or a long drive down and around the San Diego Bay, thru Imperial Beach, and up the Silver Stand. I wanted to continue on to Coronado that night but conceded to my parent's wishes. I can still remember the anxiety I felt; I couldn't wait to see the Naval Amphibious Base and surrounding area, but that would have to wait until morning. Our motel did have a swimming pool and even though it wasn't heated, I spent at least an hour swimming laps to dispel some of my pent-up energy. The pool water was cold, but I would soon find out that this was nothing compared to what awaited me in training.

We made an early start the following morning, and I couldn't get over how unique and beautiful San Diego was. The ferryboat ride to Coronado was an experience unto itself and the highlight of my arrival in Southern California. I will always cherish those trips between Coronado and San Diego. Discontinuing the ferryboat removed a vestige of the old world charm that was a mainstay of the nineteen-sixties. To this day, I look for the ferryboat when I return to Coronado, hoping that someday they may revitalize this as a means of transportation for those wishing to revisit a time when things moved just a little slower.

When we arrived at the Naval Amphibious Base, I was directed to the barracks I would temporarily call home. I would remain here until the BUDS training barracks were made ready and more trainees arrived. To me, walking through the door of the temporary barracks was like opening the gates of heaven. After a year aboard the USS *Saint Paul*, it wouldn't have taken a whole lot to make me happy, but I hadn't expected this lavishness. Here I was assigned to a cubical with three other men. Aboard ship, a space this size would have been used to accommodate twenty to twenty-five men, not four. To top it all, I was also given my very own, full standup locker to store my belongings. This wasn't at all like the *Paul* where I had stored everything I needed in a locker that was ten inches high, sixteen inches wide, and twenty-four inches deep. During that previous year, when I served aboard the *Saint Paul*, if we were in a warm climate, I would have to move all of my winter blue uniforms to my sea bag, which was then placed in the sea-bag locker. Then, when we traveled to a cold climate, I would move my blue uniforms to the locker and white uniforms to the sea bag and the sea-bag locker. Aboard ship, my locker had provided just enough room to store three uniforms and only then if they were properly folded. At this new duty station, I had entered into a whole new world, and it would take time for me to adjust, accept, and make the transition. Everything that had to do with my life was new and exciting, and I loved it.

    I had arrived a month before training was scheduled to start and this provided me with the opportunity to meet the other trainees as they arrived. This also gave me ample time to run, exercise, and prepare myself physically for the start of training. Bob Wagner had arrived a few days before I arrived and we became immediate friends. The one thing that made Bob standout from all others was his physical dominance—he was huge! The third to arrive was Gary Lanphier and soon the three of us developed a bond. Each day we ran, swam, and exercised together. Gary was a character. He was feisty as hell and always harassing someone. We soon learned that this was just Gary's nature. Gary would harass us, and we would retaliate. Then, the situation would reverse itself, and we would harass Gary, and he would retaliate. This soon became the normal way of life, and it would continue throughout training and well into the Teams. Now, I could tell you many stories about

Gary, but the pre-training story that stands out above all others is the one I will share with you now.

Gary could sleep like no one else I had ever met. Once he dozed off, it was impossible to wake him. Late one night, he returned to the barracks after a night in Coronado and a few too many beers. As was typical Gary, he raised enough hell to awaken everyone. He took great delight in doing this, and after he was satisfied that indeed everyone was awake, he turned in for the night. The next morning, we decided we would get even, but no matter what we did or how hard we tried, we couldn't wake him.

By this time, we had transferred to our training barracks, which were single-story dorm structures with bunk beds, similar to those used for basic training. The barracks set approximately twenty to twenty-five feet from the bay and directly in front of a concrete boat ramp. The tidal range was roughly five feet, so when the tide was out, the boat ramp would be exposed, and when the tide was in, the ramp would be covered by about five feet of water.

With Gary still sound asleep, I removed the mattress from the bottom bunk. Then Bob and I, plus two others, each grabbed a post of Gary's bunk bed, quietly lifted, and took it out to the boat ramp. During all of this, Gary didn't budge. We waded into the water, which was just above our knees, set the bed down, and then went back and waited for the tide to come in. We sat in front of the barracks, Gary slept soundly, and the tide rose. As the tide rose, the water started slapping against the bottom of the mattress, but still Gary slept. Soon, the water soaked thru the mattress, causing Gary to roll over into the water. The thrashing and screaming that followed was a sight to behold. We laughed, cheered, and scored Gary's overall performance a solid nine out of a possible ten. When he realized what had happened and gathered his composure, Gary swam to shore and without a word walked by us and into the barracks. This incident did little to change the way Gary dealt with us, nor did it change the way we dealt with Gary. This was the way of the Teams, and there are many more Gary Lanphier stories yet to tell.

It was now the first of March and time for our class, Class-28, to begin Basic Underwater Demolition SEAL Training. This was to be the largest class ever to begin BUDS and the first time trainees had been accepted right out of Navy Boot Camp. Prior to Class-28, all men entering BUDS had to spend at least a year in the regular Navy before transferring to training. But for now, none of that mattered. It was time, and I was anxious to begin the training I had first dreamt about when I was seven years old. But, while we all shared the same desire to succeed, it would be seventeen weeks before we would find out if we possessed what it takes to earn a berth in the Teams.

BUDS CLASSMATES
SECOND WEEKEND OF TRAINING

From left to right: Ben Scales, Nick Nickelson, and Larry "Butchie" Miller. Ben would leave the program shortly after this picture was taken. Upon completion of training, Nick would be assigned to Team-12 and Larry Team-11.

HELL WEEK:

3. GOOD ADVICE

"Tadpoles, you are all slimy tadpoles and from the looks of it, none of you have what it takes to become frogs." This was an opening remark from our welcome aboard speech and probably the kindest words we would hear spoken, by our Instructors, during the first three weeks of training. Yes, we were tadpoles, all dressed in green and wearing a helmet liner also painted green, with a number painted in white on its front and back. At this point of training, we were no more than that simple white number, and the Instructors would most often use that number when dealing with us. The reason for this was our Instructors felt we did not yet warrant, nor had we earned the right to be called by our given names.

Basic Underwater Demolition SEAL Training (BUDS) had started with a bang, the Instructors shouting orders so fast it seemed impossible to keep up with them. For those trainees who made the slightest mistake, punishment would be immediate and harsh. There were more than a few men who soon questioned their decision to enter this program, but for many others that question never entered their mind. The Instructors made one point very clear; no trainee would be allowed to quit before the beginning of Hell Week. The Instructors would drop trainees before Hell Week but again—no trainee would be allowed to quit. This meant that those men who had second thoughts would remain in BUDS for at least three weeks; Hell Week was scheduled the fourth week of training.

The first two to three days were filled with running, swimming, and Physical Training (PT) or calisthenics. For those men who had arrived just before training started, that meant sore, stiff, and aching bodies. For those who came prepared, it was still difficult, but not nearly as difficult as it was for the others. The Instructors were continually screaming, punishing, and telling trainees what was expected of them if they wanted to stay in the program.

Another fact that we quickly learned in BUDS was that a trainee is required to run everywhere he goes. Even if you were on your own time, you had better be running, unless you were being driven around the Amphibious Base. If an Instructor caught a trainee walking, there would be hell to pay. Punishment was dealt out immediately and continued for as long as the Instructor felt it was warranted, and that could be several days. It didn't take long before each trainee had a good idea of what was expected of him. We soon learned that the best thing an individual trainee could do was to become invisible. But, because that wasn't possible, the next best thing was to do what you were told, to the best of your ability, and as quickly as you could do it. Also, you were better served if you didn't get on the bad side of one of the Instructors.

By the end of the third week of training, practically every trainee was in sound physical condition and, for the vast majority, it appeared that things were starting to come together. By now, the class had been divided into seven-man boat crews, and trainees were starting to work together in these small units. We spent a good deal of time in the bay and ocean learning the intricacies of the Inflatable Boat Small (IBS). While the IBS was a wonderful tool in the water, on land it was a whole different matter. When not in the water, we were required to carry the boat on our heads. Weighing in at approximately two hundred pounds, the IBS was awkward and difficult to manage. We soon learned that we didn't manage the boat; quite the contrary, the boat managed us.

Because we were required to run everywhere we went, the same held true when we were carrying the IBS. Running caused the boat to bounce up and down, which in turn drove our necks down into our shoulders. The pain was excruciating, and there were many days I watched grown men cry, I mean literally cry like babies. The Instructors seemed to take great delight in this fact, and there were times the Instructors forced us to stand with the boat on our heads for hours on end. If by chance the boat would slip from our head to our shoulders, the Instructors would order us put a member of our boat crew in the IBS. The remaining six men would then return the boat to their heads. While this may have been great for the man in the boat, it was hell for the other members of the boat crew who were required to stand or run with the IBS on their heads.

On Saturday, the day before Hell Week was to begin, the Instructors ran the class to the Silver Strand for a special treat. Before our trip to the strand, we completed two hours of PT, but by now that was not a problem. We had been doing one to two hours of PT every day since training began, and we were ready. Few of us expected any kind of a treat from the Instructors and were, therefore, not surprised when told we would run fifteen miles in the soft sand. By soft sand, I am not talking about the sand near the beach, I am referring to the hilly sand dunes that stretched the length of the Silver Strand in the early nineteen sixties.

For some, this proved too difficult, although every man did eventually complete the run. Others were only able to finish the run with the help of members of their boat crew. Still others came to the realization that this was no longer where they wanted to be and decided they would leave the program. To quit, these trainees would simply turn in their green helmet liner the following day, Sunday, the first day of Hell Week. However, for those determined to continue, it was now time to get some sleep and dream of what awaited tomorrow.

In anticipation of Hell Week, most trainees try to find an edge that will help them overcome this major hurdle. To reach that next phase, you must first complete Hell Week, and that is much easier said than done. Finding an edge is made even more difficult because the only other men who have experienced Hell Week are those already in the Teams, and they don't talk to trainees.

However, for my class, Class-28, there was a trainee who had started training as a member of Class-27, but, due to an injury, had to drop out and was, therefore, rolled over to the next class, Class-28. His injury had occurred during the final week of training, while at San Clemente, so he knew what to expect and gave us some important advice. I should clarify that by saying he gave advice to those who wanted to be better prepared, to those who didn't, he gave nothing. But, for those who felt they were well enough prepared and didn't wish to know more, there would be severe penalties.

The trainee I refer to was Andy Anderson. He was a quiet individual who pretty much stayed to himself, but he stands alone as one of the most remarkable men to complete training. To this day, I can't imagine how he was able to go through BUDS twice, back to back, and to do so without so much as a whimper. We picked his brain as much as he would allow and came away with some rather strange suggestions. I should say, suggestions that seemed strange at the time. There were several important things that we were told to do. The first, don't wear skivvies or underpants during Hell Week. Second, shave your groin area, from your crotch down your leg, about six inches. Then, tape that area with wide white surgical tape. Now I have to admit, at that moment in time, I didn't understand or appreciate the significance of the gift I had just been given. As for most of the other trainees, they thought Andy was trying to put one over on them and most just laughed and walked away. As for me, I believed the man, and the day Hell Week was to start, I had done what had been suggested. Andy would not go into elaborate detail as to why we should do what he had suggested and pretty much left it at that.

As we started Hell Week, it didn't take long before I clearly understood the importance of what Andy had suggested. You don't wear underpants because you are wet the entire week and crawling in the sand much of that time. As you pick up sand, and it gets into your pants, it collects in the groin area and starts to rub holes in your thighs. It doesn't take long before your groin area has been rubbed raw and the underpants, if you wear them, retain the sand and exacerbate the problem. Secondly, even if you don't wear underpants, the sand in your pants collects in the groin area. Without the tape to prevent it, the sand will rub and irritate the skin and cause the area to cut and bleed. The situation became so critical for some of the trainees they could hardly walk. I would watch those men who had sustained the more severe cuts struggle to keep up with the class. Some were cut so badly that when they entered the ocean and the salt from the ocean water entered their cuts; they would suck air and grimace in pain. It's kind of like sitting in very hot water, if you have ever had that experience.

Sadly, the rash and cutting sustained by some trainees was so severe they were forced to drop out of training. I would watch others being carried along by members of their boat crew because it was too difficult for them to walk without help. There were even men who were chafed and cut so badly that the blood ran down their legs to their ankles, painting their white socks red. As hard as it was to believe, Andy's advice had saved me and the other trainees who were willing to heed his advice considerable pain.

Hell Week was but one week in training, but during that week, roughly fifty percent of the class dropped out. Not just for the reasons mentioned above, but for many and varied reasons. While physical hardship ranked high on the list, the predominant factor for men not surviving the hardship and rigors of training was due to inadequate mental preparation. As far as I was concerned, there would be nothing that could have convinced me to quit. I had wanted to be in the Teams since I was seven years old and had spent my whole life, from that point in time, with the single purpose of attaining that goal.

4. TWO NIGHTS IN HELL WEEK

The first three weeks of training are geared toward preparing each trainee for the rigors of Hell Week and the real training that is to follow. Therefore, this first phase of training is intended to build a trainee's strength and confidence and also to test his physical endurance. In addition, it is intended to provide a taste of what is to come. It is by no means easy, but it could in no way be compared to what would follow.

Then came Hell Week and six to seven days of punishment devised to weed out those trainees who did not possess the true desire and determination to continue with the even more demanding training that would follow. Whoever conjured up the name "Hell Week" could not have conceived a name more befitting this demanding period of training. Today, even after forty years, I remember this one week in my life as vividly as if it happened yesterday. And, while there were many problems or operations that Class-28 completed during this crucial week of training, there will always be two nights that, in my mind, stand out above all others.

For Class-28, Hell Week would start at one minute after midnight Sunday and continue until midnight the following Saturday or Sunday. As planned, we were introduced to Hell Week by screaming Instructors who entered our training barracks exploding M-80's (cherry bombs) and overturning bunks. As trainees spilled onto the floor, the Instructors ordered everyone outside. Then, as we walked through the door of our barracks, we were met by another group of Instructors who welcomed us with the hard blast of water from high-pressure fire hoses. It was complete pandemonium as trainees were knocked off of their feet, skidding across the ground into other trainees and knocking them to the ground. All the while, Instructors were screaming and ordering us to move to a common area between our two training barracks. Each time we tried to regain our feet, we would once again be knocked to the ground by the high-pressure water from the fire hoses. By crawling, we finally reached the common area where we were then ordered to do various calisthenics; all the while the Instructors continued to blast us with water. This continued until the Instructors were satisfied that we were ready to move to the next problem.

At this point, we were ordered back into our barracks to immediately dress and once again regroup out front. The time spent to accomplish this simple task was deemed unacceptable by the Instructors who then ordered us into the bay where we were to dog paddle and sing training-related songs for the next forty minutes. Then, because we didn't move fast enough, when ordered out of the bay, we spent the next half hour doing push-ups and more calisthenics. We were less than two hours into Hell Week, and already several trainees said they had seen enough and walked away.

Next, we formed up into two lines and ran from the Amphibious Base to the ocean, south of the Team compound, on the Silver Strand. There we were ordered to form a single line along the beach and to get on our knees. On command, we were to crawl from the beach into the water, stay for whatever period of time the Instructors felt was appropriate, and then crawl back to the beach. The Instructors would coordinate our movements through various blasts from a whistle. Upon hearing one blast from the whistle, we would start crawling into the water and continue until waves were breaking over our heads or until we had reached a point the Instructors were satisfied with. Then, two blasts from the whistle meant we were to stop crawling and remain where we were. Each time we did this seemed an eternity. Three blasts meant we were to return to the beach, at which time the Instructors would give one blast, and we would start the problem all over again. We would repeat this problem over and over, and all the while, trainees who could take no more left the program. Hard to believe, but even this early into Hell Week, many trainees were quitting.

Having completed this activity, we were once again ordered to form a straight line along the beach, at the high water line. An Instructor then walked back and forth along this line of trainees, explaining that we resembled a chain and that each man was a link in that chain. He then singled out the most senior trainee, an officer, and ordered him to lie on his back in the sand with his cap covering his face. The Instructor then told the class that this man, even though he is an officer, is no more important a link than any other link in this chain. The Instructor then ordered a seaman apprentice, the Class-28 junior trainee, to cover the officer with sand. He was given a boat paddle to complete this task and reluctantly shoveled sand on the officer, taking great care not to put sand on his face. Annoyed at this, the Instructor asked the young seaman what the hell he thought he was doing. The Instructor then grabbed the paddle from the seaman and, with considerable anger and emotion, covered the face of the officer trainee under at least two feet of sand. The Instructor then ordered the class to attention and marched us down the beach, away from the buried officer.

Everything we did in training came with a lesson, and what had happened here was no exception. This was intended to show us that in BUDS all men are treated as equals; each link is as important as the next, and this chain, Class-28, can only be as strong as each individual link. Under most circumstances in the Navy, rank has its privileges, but not here, not in BUDS. It had been quite a learning experience, and the officer who had been buried was uncovered when we were far enough down the beach to be out of sight of his unveiling. This simple maneuver, initiated by the Instructors, impacted each trainee differently; however, some were more profoundly affected than others. The enlisted man standing in front of me quit the program after seeing this, having commented, "If the Instructors would do that to our senior officer, then what do they have in store for me?"

The second incident happened the fifth night of Hell Week. It was approximately midnight when we started a night problem that required each boat crew to paddle and portage (carry) their Inflatable Boat Small (IBS) approximately twenty miles. The first leg of the exercise required each boat crew to paddle their boat down the bay from Coronado to a crossing near Imperial Beach. Each crew would then portage their IBS across the highway and sand dunes of the Silver Strand to the ocean. The boat crews would then enter the ocean and paddle back to the Naval Amphibious Base; then, finally portage each boat back across the sand dunes and highway to the starting point.

This being day five, the strain of Hell Week had taken its toll and by now, nearly half of those who started had dropped out. We were all exhausted due to lack of sleep, constantly being wet and cold, and because of the tremendous physical and mental pressure continually forced on each of us by the Instructors. Men were starting to hallucinate, some worse than others, but probably each trainee was affected in some way because of this sleep deprivation. Due to attrition, our boat crew had been reduced to five men and this only after picking up the one remaining member of a boat crew that saw six men quit the program. We were about an hour into the exercise when it happened. Four of us were paddling and Mike Paul, our boat crew officer, was aft steering. From out of nowhere, Mike screamed some incoherent words, jumped up, and dove into the water of the bay. Now, no one in his right mind would have voluntarily jumped into the water. It was terribly cold, and each of us was wet, freezing, and too miserable to do something that foolish; this hadn't been the act of a rational man. I looked at Larry Miller, another member of our boat crew, and we both laughed and then pulled Mike back into the boat. The only thing notably different was he was wide awake, but cold water does that to a person. When asked what had happened, Mike simply replied, "I saw a freight train coming straight at us and had to get out of its way."

This was day five; Hell Week would continue for another twenty-four to forty-eight hours and during this period other similar stories would unfold. Hallucinations, caused by sleep deprivation, became a common occurrence for those men who endured the rigors of Hell Week. But, for all those men who stayed the course, the feeling of accomplishment, having survived this nearly impossible milestone, is one we shall always cherish. However, this was by no means the end of training; it was only the beginning.

5. NIGHT PROBLEMS

There were many instances when, as BUDS Trainees, we were required to conduct night problems. So many in fact, that before training had ended; I felt that we trainees were nocturnal. During Hell Week, our week without sleep, we performed a never-ending array of night problems. Then, after Hell Week, we were required to perform night problems, at a minimum, two or three nights a week. This depended on the phase of training and what we were being taught during the day. For example, if we were learning to use a closed circuit unit such as the Dragger, the hands-on use of the equipment taught during the day would be put to practical use through sneak attacks at night. No matter what, the true test of all that we learned during training took place at night. Because stealth operations are most often successfully conducted at night it is said, "Frogmen rule the night." Therefore, one of the principles of training is that all trainees become as proficient and comfortable working in the darkness as in the light and develop a preference for working at night.

I think it would be safe to say that for every man who completed BUDS, there is one night problem, undertaken during training, which stands out from all others and comes to mind when the words "Night Problems" are spoken. For me that particular event occurred on the third night of Hell Week. We were to enter the ocean, just behind the Team Compound, and paddle our Inflatable Boat Small (IBS), one mile, to a rock jetty that extended out into the Ocean. This jetty consisted of huge boulders, roughly the size of a small car, and protruded fifty to seventy-five yards into the ocean from a beach near the Del Coronado Hotel.

Each boat crew was comprised of seven men, three on each side to paddle and one aft, the officer in charge of the boat crew, whose job it was to steer.

Once we had reached our objective, we were to remain in the water, between four and five hundred yards off the appointed beach, and wait for the BUDS Instructors to signal us to come ashore. We would then paddle our boat to the rocks, climb out of the boat and portage, or carry the boat across the rocks to the beach.

We had successfully completed the rock portage on several previous occasions, but each of those portages had been conducted during the day, in relatively light surf, and even then it was a difficult process. When a boat crew reaches the rocks, it is imperative that each member of the boat crew exit the IBS on the ocean side of the boat. At this point, the boat and paddles must be moved up onto the rocks, out of the surf zone, as quickly as possible. If a trainee should happen to get caught between the boat and the rocks, the force of the boat, driven by incoming waves, could crush him. Therefore, even in small surf, a rock portage is no simple matter, and the only way to successfully complete this operation is through teamwork and the trust and confidence that each member of the boat crew thoroughly understands and will successfully complete his assigned task.

It was probably nineteen hundred hours or seven in the evening when we entered the water to start the operation. It was cold, and the surf was booming. When I say booming, I am not referring to waves that are six to eight feet high, I mean more in the neighborhood of twelve to fifteen feet. Huge waves that you know can cause serious damage and pain if you screw up. The night was overcast, cloudy, and therefore very dark. You could hear the waves when they crashed on the beach, but it was too dark to see them clearly. You knew they were huge from the roar they made as they slammed onto the beach, a clear indication we were in for a rough ride. As we waded into the water, I heard Larry "Butchie" Miller, a true operator and member of my boat crew shout, "Look

Out." A boat crew that had entered the water, a few seconds before us, had been lifted about fifteen feet into the air by one of these huge waves, turned upside down, and the men and boat then slammed onto the beach with such force that it broke one of the trainee's paddles. I could hear another trainee sucking for air; he was making that distinct sound one makes when his wind has been knocked out. Luckily, that was all that happened and they picked themselves up, gathered their composure, and started back into the water to try once again to make it past the surf zone.

Each boat crew would be dumped at least once by those huge waves, others several times, and for a while it seemed that we might spend the entire night just trying to clear the surf zone. Eventually, as our IBS slid over the final swell and the boat crew settled into the routine of paddling toward the objective, I began thinking about the rock portage that awaited us. If it had been difficult to successfully complete the portage during the day, when the surf was small, what would it be like at night when the surf was booming? Time moved quickly, and before I knew it, we were offshore near the rocks, gathering with the other boat crews, awaiting the signal from our Instructors to come ashore and start the rock portage. It had been prearranged that the Instructors would wave a lantern as a signal for us to start paddling to the rocks and conduct the portage. For now, all of the boat crews huddled together and the trainees just looked at each other, eyes wide and terror stricken. Just thinking about making a portage in this killer surf was enough to turn your blood cold.

The swells under our boats were huge and served further warning of what was to come. From our vantage point, we could see white water jetting into the air as the surf pounded the jetty. The noise, caused by the waves breaking onto the rocks, was deafening and only lead to further uncertainty. All we could do now was settle in and wait. We sat there in silence for what seemed an eternity; then finally, there appeared a white light moving back and forth on the rocks. Red would have been our signal that the operation had been cancelled; white meant it was a go. God help us, it really wasn't red; it was white, and that meant the portage was on. We looked at each other in disbelief. Some of the men were saying it was too dangerous and were questioning whether we shouldn't all turn around and go back to the staging area where we started. I heard another trainee say he didn't want to risk death by being bashed against the rocks and others agreed. By now, all of the boat crews were talking amongst themselves, trying to figure out what would be the best thing to do; everyone that is except Mike Paul, the officer in charge of our boat crew. "HELL YES," he shouted, then "HOOYAH," and before I knew what had happened we were paddling like crazy. The men from the other boat crews looked on in astonishment as we headed toward the rock jetty. Now I don't mind saying that I said several prayers on the way to the rocks, and I can assure you that I wasn't alone. We paddled feverishly, the other boat crews sat there in total disbelief, and we tried to remain focused.

    Soon, we could see the huge waves pounding the rocks. It was as if nature was showing what she had in store for us. As we drew closer, I could more clearly see the light on the rocks and drew confidence from the fact that our Instructors always knew what was best for us and wouldn't expose us to a situation we wouldn't be able to handle. However, once again I said a prayer that we would all make it safely. The two previous times we had attempted a rock portage, during the day, the surf deposited our boat at the base of the rocks, and we jumped out, climbed the rocks, pushing and pulling our IBS, hoping the waves that followed would help by further pushing our boat along and thus helping us lift it onto the rocks. Not this time, as we came closer to the rock jetty, what must have been the wave of all waves caught our boat, lifting it high into the air and pushing us forward faster and faster. Then, before I knew what had happened, the wave broke and we were deposited right on top of the rocks, not below or beside the jetty, as had been the case during our previous portages. We looked at each other in total disbelief and then quickly jumped out of our IBS and spilled what water was inside. We then moved quickly across the rocks and to the beach before the next wave arrived. I am certain that the adrenalin rush we each experienced gave us the extra energy and strength needed to move the boat as quickly as we did.

On the beach, some very anxious Instructors greeted us. They had called the exercise off because of the huge surf. None of the other boat crews had attempted the portage, only ours. Apparently, after we had started paddling to the rocks, the Instructors had hoisted the red lantern. We had been so busy paddling and concentrating on our objective that we hadn't noticed. In reality, there was no way for us to have known, because the Instructors were waving the lantern from beside the rocks, not on them. But what about the white light that had signaled us to come ashore? It had certainly been there; we had scrambled past it when transferring our boat from the rocks to the beach, although we weren't thinking about the light while dragging our boat off of the jetty. We were then told that the light had come from a flashlight, used by a man looking for crabs; it hadn't been the signal to come ashore from one of the Instructors. As I looked back at the rock jetty and the man who was still out there looking for crabs, I thought about what could have happened, but those thoughts soon faded. For a short while, our boat crew was heralded by the Instructors for willingly undertaking what we felt we had been directed to do while the other boat crews had hesitated. In reality, the other Trainees had made the right decision. Had they followed our lead, and all paddled to the rock jetty, men might have been severely injured, even killed. This night operation had ended in our favor. We had succeeded, but we had also been lucky.

6. LAST MAN STANDING

While Hell Week provided a long list of memories, one that ranks high on that list relates to the time our class, Class-28, spent at the "Mudflats." Mudflats, in actuality it was a waste depository for the base hospital as well as a reservoir of soupy sludge, located on the Bay side of the Silver Strand, south of Coronado.

The mudflats has a distinct odor, similar to but more pungent than rotten eggs, and serves but one purpose, training those individuals aspiring to enter the ranks of UDT/SEAL Teams. There is a reason for training in the mudflats, just as there is a reason for everything we did during Hell Week, or for that matter, BUDS. Apparently, during the Korean War, frogmen were required to swim up rivers that were filled with dead and decomposing bodies. As you might imagine, the stench was horrible, and some of the men found it difficult to function under these conditions. However, they did what had to be done and learned to acclimate themselves to these adverse conditions. After the Korean War, it was decided that BUDS training required an element that exposed trainees to similar conditions. The mudflats would be well suited to fulfill that need.

It was day three when we launched our "Inflatable Boat Small" (IBS) into the bay and struck out for the mudflats. During Hell Week, your IBS goes with you practically everywhere you go. The IBS is extremely important because it is one of the more frequent means by which men are deployed or inserted into a combat area. It is also your lifeline when leaving a hostile beach for your mother ship or submarine. Therefore, the Instructors expect you to develop a love affair with your IBS and to treat her better than you would your wife or girlfriend. Today, more sophisticated equipment, has to a large extent, replaced the IBS, but it still has its place in BUDS training and the Teams.

During Training, as well as in the Teams, a boat crew is comprised of seven men, three on each side to paddle and a coxswain at the rear to steer. When not in the water, the seven men portage, or carry on their heads, the IBS to move it across land. Weighing nearly two hundred pounds, the boat is unruly, heavy, and not easy to master. Now I said seven-men per boat crew, but in actuality, by the third day of Hell Week, many boat crews averaged five men. As men quit and the size of boat crews grew ever smaller, never below five however, Instructors shuffled men, adding to or eliminating boat crews. This was a never-ending problem, due to the high attrition, that continued thru Hell Week.

As we paddled toward our objective, the stench of the mudflats caught our attention long before we actually arrived. As we drew closer, we could see the Instructors standing on top of sand dunes that flank the mudflats. Upon arrival, we were ordered to beach our boats and to fall in at attention. The Instructors then ordered us to get acquainted with this lovely spot we would call home, until they felt we earned the right to leave. With that, we waded into the mud, which is roughly waist deep. That angered the Instructors who then ordered us to dive into the mud. We did as we were ordered and thus began a series of exercises devised by the Instructors. These included calisthenics and seeing who could stay completely submerged, under the mud, for the longest period of time. By now we were totally immersed in the muck and to the delight of the Instructors, the fun began.

During Hell Week, each boat crew competes against the other boat crews. Every problem or exercise, assigned by the Instructors, is awarded points. If your boat crew finishes first, you receive the most points, second fewer, and so on. However, the last two boat crews to finish a problem receive no points or have points deducted from the points they had previously earned. There is a purpose to this apparent madness of awarding points. The boat crew that accumulates the most points is exempt from a portion of the final day of Hell Week. That alone makes acquiring the maximum number of points, in each problem or exercise, a reason to excel in every aspect of Hell Week.

For the next several hours, boat crew competed against boat crew in various exercises ordained by the Instructors. Then we were told that it was lunchtime and that we were to take a seat in the mud. Here we sat, covered with mud from head to toe, as the Instructors started throwing box lunches to the class. The mud did not serve as a deterrent, and we ate our lunch with much enthusiasm, mud and all. When finished, the Instructors told us that they had something "special" in store for us. Whenever you heard the word "special," you knew you were in for something all right, but it would in no way be special.

We were ordered out of the mud and to the top of one of the sand dunes. Then, one of the boats was overturned at the edge of the mudflats, near the bottom of the dune. The Instructors ordered us to assemble as boat crews and then, one man at a time, run down the sand dune and dive into the mud. The IBS would serve as the platform to dive from. The performance of our dive would be judged and scored by the Instructors and points awarded based on performance. You know, similar to scoring Olympic diving.

With that we started the mud dives for glory and points. Who would be the most prolific mud diver, and who would be responsible for adding points to his boat crew's standing? Now, if you performed a lousy dive, you were reprimanded and ordered to complete various exercises, in the mud. You were then excluded from further competition, therefore sitting in the mud only able to observe. But, if you performed a satisfactory dive, approved and appreciated by the Instructors, you were allowed to dive again. Some of the divers were actually stuck waist deep, head first, in the muck. If it weren't for another trainee jumping in to pull the man out, he would have suffocated. Once in that muck, it became impossible for a trainee to extract himself without the help of another.

Time after time, the winners went back up the hill to jump again and again. Before long, most trainees came to the realization that winning the diving contest wasn't everything it had been built up to be. So, instead of punishing oneself in a grueling feat that would conclude with one man standing, most performed an unimpressive dive, took their punishment, and retired to the spectator seats in the mud. One thing you should know, if the Instructors felt you were not putting forth one hundred percent on each dive, you would be in for untold punishment dealt at their hands.

The diving contest went on for several hours before a winner was finally declared. We then went back to compete in countless mud-related exercises that continued until the sun started to go down. At this point, we were ordered into the bay to wash the mud off as best we could and then to paddle our boats back to our training area. At our barracks, we were allowed to take a shower and change into clean fatigues. We found that the stench of the mudflats had not only permeated our clothing but also our skin as well, making it impossible to wash off, no matter how hard we tried. It would be at least a week before the smell of the mudflats finally dissipated from our bodies. As for the clothes we wore that day, we were ordered to throw them in the dumpster. The Instructors knew that the smell of the mudflats could never be removed from the clothing.

After showering and changing into dry fatigues, we were ordered to fall in outside of our barracks. From there, we were ordered into the bay where we dog-paddled and sang songs for about an hour. We then formed up and ran to the mess hall for dinner, prior to starting our next night problem. We were not yet half way through Hell Week but had already spent roughly sixty-eight hours of this training cycle without sleep.

While I can recall many aspects of Hell Week, I cannot recall the name of the man who won the diving contest, the man who won the enviable title "The last man standing" from Class-28. I do know that after our day in the mud, each day of Hell Week became ever harder, never easier, and I guess that is why they say, "During BUDS, the only easy day was yesterday."

A trainee sitting in the mud waiting to receive his box lunch.

A trainee runs from the top of the sand dunes, jumps onto the overturned Inflatable Boat Small (IBS), and is then propelled into the air and mud.

Trainee on right jumps in to pull trainee on left from the mud. Without help, it would not be possible to extract yourself from the mud.

Trainee Gary Lanphier pulling fellow trainee from mud as Instructors look on.

7. CHECKING IN

It was the third night of Hell Week, and by now roughly one-third of those men who had started BUDS Class-28 had dropped out, unable to deal with the rigors of training. For those who remained, far fewer than half would see it through to completion. But the focus this night would be on completing the operation or problem at hand, for in BUDS you learn to deal with one minute at a time, one hour at a time, and one problem at a time. Thinking of completing training and taking an assignment in the Teams was reserved for the last day of training, and that was months away.

It was approximately twenty-two hundred hours, or ten at night, when Class-28 formed up in front of our training barracks. We had just successfully completed a night problem at the rock jetty near the Hotel Del Coronado. There was little time for rest as we geared up and prepared our boat for the next training exercise. This night problem would require each boat crew to paddle their Inflatable Boat Small (IBS) roughly ten miles, or the length of the bay, from Coronado to Imperial Beach. We would then cross the Strand that separates the bay from the ocean, enter the Ocean, and paddle our boats back to Coronado. Once this was accomplished, the Instructors would then assign the next of as many night problems as would be required to get us through to morning and the start of day training exercises.

When the Instructors ordered the class to start the exercise, ours was the first boat to enter the water. We then paddled our boat as hard as we could in order to get out in front of the other boat crews. We were competing against them for much cherished points that are awarded the first crews to complete each problem or exercise. The competition for points would culminate the final day of Hell Week, and the boat crew with the most points would be excluded from a portion of the problems conducted on that final day or night. So as you can imagine, every exercise, operation, or problem conducted during Hell Week was critically important.

For this particular night problem the Instructors had devised a way to prevent boat crews from taking shortcuts and crossing the Strand, say at two miles, instead of the planned ten miles. Every two to three miles an Instructor would set-up a "check-in station." Then, as a boat crew reached each check-in station, the boat would pause for a moment and a member of that boat crew would shout out the number assigned to their particular boat. After the Instructor acknowledged that the boat crew had properly checked in, that boat could then move on to the second check-in station and so on.

It was now past twenty-two hundred hours, overcast and because there was no moon to light up the beach, it was difficult to see the first check-in station and impossible to see the Instructors who were supposed to be on the beach. In addition, the distance between the Instructors on the beach and the boats in the water was roughly three hundred yards, and that added to the difficulty of seeing anything.

We reached the first scheduled check-in station far ahead of the other boats, but there was no response to our shouts. Apparently, the Instructors had not yet arrived. We waited as precious minutes passed, knowing our lead was diminishing as the other boat crews drew nearer. Five minutes, still no sign of the Instructors, where could they be? As the other boat crews closed in, Mike Paul, the coxswain and officer in charge of our boat crew, ordered us to paddle to the beach. When we reached the beach there were no Instructors so we pulled our boat out of the water, sat down on the sand, and waited.

Then it happened. The second boat arrived and the coxswain shouted out "SEVEN" their boat number. At that, Mr. Paul shouted back, "Boat Crew number seven, O.K., proceed to check point number two." They then started paddling, on their way to the second check-in station. Then another boat arrived and another and all the while Mr. Paul continued sending them happily on their way. The Instructors arrived just as Mr. Paul approved the last boat's passage. When asked why we were on the beach and not in the water, Mike simply informed the Instructor that we knew we shouldn't go on to the second check-in station without clearing the first; and, because it was impossible to see anything on the beach, we had come ashore. With that, the Instructor gave his approval and sent us on our way.

As we were walking our boat into the water, the Instructor asked if any of the other boats had passed. To that, Mr. Paul responded that the other boat crews had decided not to wait, as we had, and, therefore, went ahead to the second check-in station. The Instructor then told us to wait as he called ahead to speak to his counterpart at check-in station number two. At this point, my heart started to pound because I knew the Instructor would soon find out what we had done. Then, the only thing left would be deciding the punishment befitting such a breech of protocol. Mike just smiled and told us to be calm and not to worry because everything was under control.

It took another ten minutes before we heard again from the Instructor. Apparently, the other crews were called ashore and chastised for not reporting in at the first checkpoint. Each crew swore they had checked in at the first check-in station and it didn't take long for the Instructors to figure out what had happened. Then, to my surprise, we were not punished. To the contrary, the Instructors thought what Mr. Paul had pulled off was inspirational and the Instructor who had been dealing with us stood about twenty feet away having a good laugh. The Instructor then ordered us to get the hell out of his sight, and we made a mad scramble for our boat and the water.

As we were making our way to the second check-in station, we started to pass the other boats paddling toward us. They were on their way back to the first station to check in again, but this time it would be for real. We heard some very strong and disparaging language as each crew passed us, but that was not important because for this operation we were unbeatable. We successfully completed the exercise, far ahead of the others, and thanks to Mr. Paul, we were awarded double points for what he had done. The other boat crews were then informed that, in the future, Mr. Paul should be referred to as the master of, "Checking-In."

8. A FREE RIDE

While much has been written about Hell Week, it seems that there is always one more story that begs to be told. And, for those trainees who survived this week of Hell, Hell Week will provide many unforgettable memories. During Hell Week, there are no gifts, no easy times, no fun times, and certainly no free rides. Or, is there? I can recall one instance when a member of the boat crew, to which I was assigned, actually received a free ride. Much to our dismay, this would come at the expense of the other members of our boat crew.

It was the fourth morning of Hell Week, and we had already spent several hours at the obstacle course. The course is comprised of approximately twenty obstacles, each one harder than the last. This is another way for the Instructors to determine which trainees have the heart and desire to continue and which do not. The obstacle course had been designed to make it extremely difficult to complete every obstacle without making a mistake. Mistakes then led to punishment at the hands of the Instructors. For those who did navigate the course successfully, the Instructors would look at the time it took the trainee to complete the course and then use his time against him. Basically, it was impossible to complete the course to the Instructors' satisfaction. But the main thing to remember is the fact that it is the boat crew, not the individual, that receives the grade for how well the obstacle course is completed. You are, therefore, only as strong as the weakest member of your boat crew.

As was mentioned earlier, during Hell Week you compete as a boat crew against all other boat crews. Points are awarded if you do well and deducted if you do poorly. Therefore, when a member of your boat crew screws up, every member of your boat crew is punished. If a single member of your boat crew does poorly on the obstacle course, the entire boat crew must suffer. Punishment most assuredly means you will all be required to spend some time in the cold water of the Pacific Ocean. It also means that you will be required to conduct physical training (P.T.), including a series of exercises with a waterlogged telephone pole, and those exercises will be done in the ocean shallows or nearby sand. You do these exercises until you feel your arms are going to drop off and you cannot possibly do them any longer. Then, when the Instructors are satisfied that you have been punished sufficiently, you go back to the obstacle course to start again. By this time, you are so exhausted you can only do worse than you had previously done, so you receive further punishment. Before long, each boat crew is in the same fix, and everyone is being punished. In reality, this is the way the Instructors intended it to be.

At this point of Hell Week, men are dropping like flies. Many find it much easier to quit than to continue. One of the major contributors to this is hypothermia. A trainee is constantly wet and cold, and there is nothing he can do to prevent it. Again, this is the way the Instructors intend it to be, and from this they will determine just how far each trainee can be pushed before breaking and which are the men with that extra something that prevents him from quitting?

Another problem that comes into play is the sand. Because you are wet and continually crawling in the sand, you are covered with it, both on the inside of your clothes as well as on the outside. You collect sand in your groin area, as well as your socks around your ankles. (In case you didn't know, this is the reason few men in the Teams wear skivvies, underpants, shorts, briefs, or whatever you call them.) It's been so long since I wore them, I can't recall. After a while the sand starts to cut and chafe, and there is nothing you can do to prevent this from happening. Over time, the cuts become so bad that, in some cases, merely walking is torture. In several instances, I saw trainees whose socks were blood red from serious cuts that resulted from this chafing. Then, when these men entered the ocean and the salt water came into contact with their cuts and abrasions, you could see them languish in pain. If you have ever seen someone sit in extremely hot water and heard the sound that they make as they suck in their breath from the pain, you will know what I mean. That is the sound made by these men. For many, it became so unbearable that they were forced to quit the program. For others, it didn't matter; they wouldn't quit no matter how bad their cuts or how severe the pain.

We continued performing exercises and enduring punishment, at the obstacle course, until noon. Each boat crew was then ordered to lift and place, on their heads, their IBS. The Inflatable Boat Small (IBS) accompanies each boat crew practically everywhere that crew goes during Hell Week. The boat weighs nearly two hundred pounds and is manned by a boat crew of seven men. During Hell Week, the standard compliment of a boat crew varies as men quit, but probably averages closer to five. When you are not in the water, you carry the boat on your head wherever you go. When the Instructors order you to "Head Carry," you then lift and place the boat on your head and await further orders. Now, there is no way I can explain the pain associated with carrying this boat on your head. It is difficult with seven men, but it becomes nearly impossible with five. You position men by height and do the best to distribute the weight of the boat equally, but that is much more difficult than it sounds. Walking is difficult enough, but when you are forced to run, and the boat is bouncing up and down, driving your neck down into your shoulders, it becomes almost unbearable. Throughout training, you never walk; you run everywhere you go, so I think you can see what I am getting at.

As our boat crew was going to the head-carry position, Mr. Paul, the Officer in charge of our boat crew and also our boat coxswain, made some smart remark to Doc. Barber, one of our Instructors. Don't ask me why, because Barber was an individual capable of bringing undue punishment upon the members of our boat crew. This wasn't the first, nor would it be the last time that Mike's off-the-wall comments would cause us unimaginable but avoidable pain. The truth is Doc. Barber truly liked Mr. Paul, but he enjoyed punishing us for the things Mike did, and this time was no different.

At this juncture of training, our boat crew consisted of six men, five enlisted and one officer, Mr. Paul. One of the enlisted men named Tom, a second class petty officer, stood about six feet tall and weighed about two hundred twenty pounds. He was muscular and had the look of a person who belonged in the Teams. The other members of the boat crew were of average build but were very capable of carrying their own weight. Larry "Butchie" Miller, Mike Paul, and I were all members of the original boat crew, but due to attrition, new members were added as others quit. Larry and I worked well together, and he was the one person I could always count on when things got tough. And, right now things were about to get really tough because Doc. Barber had devised a way to punish us for the comment Mr. Paul had made earlier.

Doc. Barber then smiled and told Tom, the heaviest member of our boat crew, to get into our IBS. He then ordered the remaining five of us to lift the boat onto our heads. We all looked at each other and then did as we were ordered. I should say we tried to do as we were ordered. We found it nearly impossible to lift the boat; it was awkward and shifted from side to side with the extra weight of the man inside. When we did finally manage to raise the boat to our heads, Doc. Barber told Mr. Paul to come out from under the boat to join him. Then, with Tom in the boat, and the boat on our heads, the four of us were ordered to run from the Strand to the mess hall, a distance of roughly one-half mile.

There is no way to explain the pain we experienced during that run from the Strand to the mess hall. When the head and neck pain became too excruciating, we would try to carry the boat on our shoulders, but that did little to help. For each step we took, the boat became heavier, and moving the IBS from head to shoulder and back became ever harder. The pain that I felt was like nothing I had experienced to that point in training. And, all the time we were moving toward the mess hall, the finish line, I could see Mr. Paul jogging along with Doc. Barber, not helping, or sharing in the punishment he had been responsible for inflicting upon us.

When we did reach the mess hall, we dumped the boat, Tom and all, and the four of us fell to the ground, too fatigued to go in and eat. Then the unexpected happened, Tom looked at us and calmly announced that he was quitting the program. He had decided this while riding in the boat on the way back from the Strand. Larry and I looked at each other, but we were too stunned and exhausted to do anything when we heard this. I didn't know if I was angrier with Tom for quitting or with Mr. Paul for putting us in this predicament. I do know that I would have been better prepared if one of the other members of our boat crew, who had actually carried the boat, had been the one to inform us that he was quitting. Another thing, if Tom had quit when we were still at the obstacle course, or even on the way back, it would have changed all that had transpired. Doc. Barber would have been busy dealing with Tom leaving the program and, therefore, would have had to postpone our punishment until later. But still another way to look at it, had the punishment been postponed until later, it could have been worse, but that seems unlikely. However, to this day, there is one thing that I am certain of: During the training of Class-28, Tom was the only man given, "A free ride."

Trainees exercising with waterlogged telephone pole.

This picture shows a boat crew trying to paddle their Inflatable Boat Small (IBS) thru the surf. In this case the Instructors had the trainees turn their boat upside down to make the paddle more difficult. More difficult, that's an understatement, try impossible.

9. MUTE SCREAMS AND JELLY BEANS

It was twenty-two hundred hours or ten p.m., the fourth night of Hell Week, and we were cold and exhausted. During the previous four days, we had been conducting exercise after training exercise, twenty-four hours a day, without an hour's sleep. But, each day, during the previous three days, we had been given a thirty to forty-five minute break. This wasn't nearly enough time to even think about sleep, so we spent it trying to get warm. When we were given the first break, most trainees changed into dry clothes, without anticipating the consequences. When the Instructors saw this, they immediately ordered everyone into the cold water of the bay, and there we stayed for the next half hour. Thus, we learned that changing into dry clothes was a waste of time and avoided doing so from that point forward. From the first, until the last minute of Hell Week, we were wet and cold. That is the way it had been planned by our Instructors, and that is the way it was carried out.

We had just completed our evening training exercise, much to the dissatisfaction of the Instructors, when we were ordered to assemble in front of our barracks. Our training compound and barracks were directly across from and very near the bay. As punishment for not doing what would have been deemed satisfactory, we were ordered into the bay. There we would stay until the Instructors were satisfied that we had paid for our transgressions.

In order to survive Basic Underwater Demolition SEAL Training (BUDS), you must learn one basic precept. When it seems that you can't take any more, you must retreat to a place in your mind, totally separate and away from the situation at hand. I don't mean to avoid the situation, but you must learn how to avoid letting it take control; you must be its master. One way to do this is to sing. May sound strange, but during training, you do a lot of singing, it helps take your mind off of your suffering. Also, when you hear the voices of the other trainees, you realize that you are not in it alone, the only one feeling pain. The songs that you sing are not top ten tunes but rather, silly songs, fraternity songs, songs without meaning. If a trainee knows one, he then teaches the others. Just the simple task of learning the song helps take your mind off of your suffering.

So, here we were in the bay, dog-paddling and singing songs. Thirty, then forty-five minutes elapsed, and the thought that we wouldn't be given the break we had been so anxiously anticipating, started to control my thoughts. Had the Instructors been so disappointed with our performance that there would be no break? I just didn't know.

Then came what we had all been hoping for, a signal from the Instructors telling us to leave the water. At this point, all I could think about was trying to get warm, finding a way to stop shaking, a way to put heat back into my freezing body. As the trainees struggled out of the water, one of the Instructors shouted, "You have forty-five minutes, don't waste them, ladies." It would be a mad dash for the showers and then forty-five minutes of standing under the hot water in an effort to replenish the body heat lost during that grueling day. This was foremost in everyone's mind. By now, we knew it would be wasted effort to change into something dry, so we would remain in our clothes and enjoy standing under a hot shower.

As we were climbing out of the water, Doc Barber, one of the Instructors, asked Mike Paul, our boat crew officer, if he would like some jellybeans. Barber had been eating jellybeans and harassing us the whole time we had been in the bay. Now, everything that you do during Hell Week is done as a boat crew, a team, not as an individual. Therefore, if one person in the boat crew screws up, the whole boat crew is punished, not just the individual. I say this because what was to happen next would bring pain, not only to Mr. Paul, but to the four members of his boat crew as well. In response to Doc Barber's question, Mr. Paul loudly replied, "Hey Doc Barber, only candy asses eat jellybeans!" Now, can you imagine what went thru my mind when I heard this? This was not the typical response made to an Instructor during training, but especially not when the training class had just been awarded a break, a chance to get out of the freezing water and under a hot shower. Doc. Barber then asked Mr. Paul if he had heard him correctly. Before any of us could intervene, Mike repeated, "I said, only candy asses eat jellybeans." It had happened so quickly that none of us had a chance to stop him. I looked at Larry Miller, and he looked at me, neither of us could believe what had just happened. By now, all of the other trainees who had heard Mr. Paul started scrambling over each other, doing everything in their power to distance themselves from us. You know that old adage, "guilt by association." Well, I'm certain they knew there would be sever repercussions for what Mike had said, and none of them wanted to be a part of it. But for us, it was too late; we stood there frozen in time, still trying to comprehend the magnitude of what had just happened.

  Doc. Barber laughed, and for a moment I thought everything would be all right. That feeling vanished in a heartbeat as I heard Doc. Barber tell Mr. Paul that he had "Something Very Special in store for him." We all knew "him" really meant "us" and whatever it was, it wasn't going to be a nice kind of special. I was so cold I had to concentrate in order to talk and when I did, the words were barely audible. I wanted to shout at Mr. Paul, but I couldn't and besides, I was more concerned with the "Something Very Special" that Doc Barber had promised.

  Now, the last thing that any of us wanted to do was to get back into the cold water. Therefore, I shouldn't have been surprised when asked, "what is the one thing you would least like to do?" and Mike responded, "spend any more time in the bay." Anyone, especially an officer, should have known that the answer to that question could dictate the, "Something Very Special" Doc Barber had in mind. Why couldn't Mike have said, take a hot shower or, find some nice warm place to rest. Now mind you, I'm not saying the latter would have redirected the inevitable decision made by Doc Barber, but the use of a little psychology might have prevented our spending the next forty-five minutes in the cold water.

With that, Larry and I turned around and jumped back into the bay, anticipating the inevitable, and rightly so. Doc. Barber laughed and told Mike and the rest of the boat crew to do the same. All I could think about was strangling Mr. Paul, as we dog-paddled and Doc. Barber sat there eating his jellybeans. I tried to talk to Mike but was so cold I could barely get the words out. We tried to sing but were too cold for that as well. I thought about the other trainees standing under the hot shower and became more enraged at Mike. Then again, Doc. Barber asked Mr. Paul if he would like some jellybeans. At this point, I tried to scream, but nothing happened. I was so cold my words were inaudible. Luckily, Mr. Paul didn't respond to Barber's request, and our punishment ended when the rest of our class was ordered to fall in and start the next training exercise. You guessed it, forty-five minutes later.

The time period, during which the above transpired, was no more than two hours. A mere two hours of all those hours that comprised Hell Week. And, while this may not be an event remembered by other members of Class 28, for me, it left a lasting impression. Many years have passed since that fateful night, but to this very day, whenever I see jellybeans or hear of someone screaming and not being heard, I am always drawn back to that night of "Mute Screams and Jellybeans."

POST HELL WEEK TRAINING:

10. DO YOU WANT TO QUIT?

During Basic Underwater demolition SEAL Training (BUDS), it is the Instructors job to push each trainee to his limit; it is also the job of the Instructor to ferret out any weakness a trainee may possess and then exploit that weakness. Therefore, if you possess such a flaw, something that truly bothers you, you would be well advised to bury it and not let it become known to the Instructors. The one thing you can count on is if an Instructor does find out about that weakness, it will be used against you. In addition, you would be better served to keep it from your fellow classmates as well. Not saying they would, but they might accidentally slip this information to the Instructors.

The one question most often asked trainees by their Instructors is "Do You Want To Quit?" Of course the answer to this question is a no brainer, unless quitting is truly your intent and you have decided that you want no more of the Instructors' punishment or the rigors of training. If it is your desire to quit, then you simply withdrew to the area designated for those who have gone before you, place your helmet liner on the ground, next to all those helmet liners of trainees who have previously left the program, and it's over. At this point, you are immediately escorted from the BUDS training area never to be heard from or seen again. The purpose for this immediate transition from BUDS to a fleet assignment is so that those who quit will in no way be exposed to or negatively influence those trainees continuing with the program.

Each morning we would muster in front of our training barracks before going to the practice field for Physical Training (PT). One morning, as we stood at attention in front of our barracks, an Instructor shouted, "If anyone here wants to quit, take one step forward." Gary Lanphier, a trainee and member of Class-28, was standing in the front row at the time this question was asked. Ron Tussi, another trainee standing in the second row, put a foot in Gary's back and gave him a hearty shove. With that, Gary was not only in front of the class, but he was half way down the road to hell and only seconds away from receiving extreme punishment at the hands of the Instructors. The Instructors immediately swarmed down on Gary and were unsympathetic to his denials, as he struggled to get back in line. Though Gary tried, the Instructors refused to hear his pleas that he had been pushed out of line by one of his classmates. This was a major infraction and cause for punishment from Instructors who knew well how to handle such a situation. But, before I go much further, I should tell you a little about Gary.

Gary Lanphier was the Class-28 trainee most singled out by Instructors and Trainees alike for daily punishment and harassment. Gary was of average height, slightly overweight, and when he ran, his knees almost knocked together. By looking at Gary, you might surmise that he had not even a remote chance of making it thru BUDS. However, housed within that somewhat unorthodox frame was the heart of a lion, and that heart permitted Gary to take whatever punishment or harassment was inflicted upon him by either the Instructors or his fellow trainees. It seemed that the more punishment the Instructors dished out, and believe me it was considerable, the tougher Gary became. In addition, as if life weren't difficult enough, the vast majority of Class-28 trainees also harassed Gary. Don't ask me why, at the time it simply seemed like the right thing to do, and it was fun. However, if you were a trainee involved in harassing Gary, the one thing that you could count on was retaliation. Gary was not a person to go softly into the night; he made sure you paid double for any pain you inflicted, or were responsible for others inflicting upon him. However, just the pleasure of getting Gary made retaliation seem unimportant at the time, and retaliation was an acceptable byproduct for some of the hell we put him through. Though it may sound sadistic, we took great pleasure in getting Gary, and you can believe me when I say that Gary was more often the initiator of harassment imposed on fellow trainees than he was the recipient. This harassment of and by Gary started before training actually began and continued until graduation and then even into the Teams. For Class-28, there was great satisfaction in harassing Gary and, believe it or not, seeing someone suffer more than you were suffering made training a little more bearable. Because of this simple fact, you might say that harassing Gary even helped some of the trainees make it through BUDS.

That brings us back to Gary's predicament and the forthcoming wrath the instructors were about to bestow upon Gary who now stood in front of the class. In all honesty, I don't believe the Instructors doubted the fact that Gary had been pushed, but at this point, that didn't matter. It had happened, and Ron hadn't stepped up to tell the Instructors that he was the perpetrator; therefore, Gary was to suffer the consequences. Adding to the situation was the fact that Gary was from the same hometown, Lingle, Wyoming, as one of the senior BUDS Training Officers. Now, if you think that having an Instructor from his hometown would be in Gary's favor, think again. Max Stevenson, whom I refer to, was a huge man and tougher than nails. He was built like a Greek god, and one could only imagine what would happen if he ever decided to hit you. Max also felt that Gary should be ridden as hard as a Lingle bull in order to make him quit, but as I mentioned earlier, trying to make Gary quit only strengthened his resolve to complete training.

Gary was immediately put into the push-up position and with an Instructor standing on his back, Gary was ordered to do fifty push-ups. I don't recall how many push-ups he had completed when the Instructor started to do a little dance, while still on Gary's back. As Gary lay flat on the ground, Max came running down the line and took charge of the situation. For the next fifteen minutes, he stood there verbally abusing Gary while ordering him do every imaginable exercise, one immediately following the last. Then, because Max was totally dissatisfied with his performance, Gary was ordered into the bay where he dog paddled for another ten minutes while singing songs to the delight of Instructors and trainees alike. This was great for the rest of Class-28; we just had to stand there and watch, a rare break from the rigors of training. At this point, Gary was ordered back into formation, and an Instructor ordered us to attention. Again, the Instructor shouted, "If anyone here wants to quit, take one step forward." Gary was tired, wet, and cold, but he did not budge and made sure no one pushed him this time. With that, we were marched to the training field for our daily ration of Physical Training (P.T.) or calisthenics.

I don't recall what Gary did to Ron, in retaliation for what had happened, but I do know that Gary did get even; he always evened the score. Gary would go on to graduate from BUDS and then spend the remainder of his enlistment as a member of UDT-12. He was and will always be one person that stands out from all others because of his unquestionable desire and unwillingness to be beaten. He has today, as he did during training, the heart of a true champion.

11. COLD TESTED

Have you ever heard that old axiom "He is shaking like a dog shitting peach seeds"? That saying applies to every man who has ever completed Basic Underwater Demolition SEAL (BUDS) Training. Not because he was forced to eat peaches whole, seed and all, but because of the cold, and the shivering and shaking that accompanies being very cold. This is a way of life for BUDS Trainees and if you can't handle the cold, then you would be better off staying in the regular Navy or joining one of the other branches of the military.

During BUDS, one of the primary objectives of the Instructors is to see how well each trainee copes with being cold. Each man is different; therefore, each man's tolerance level, when dealing with being cold and hypothermic, is also different. However, as a trainee, the one thing you can count on is being cold tested, and then cold tested, and finally, cold tested.

When I look back on BUDS Training, I can recall very few times when I wasn't wet and cold. It seems as though the Instructors had an aversion to seeing trainees in dry clothes; therefore, we were wet most of the time. Now, it is a simple fact of nature that when you are wet and cold, you lose body heat. Eventually, you will start to shiver and shake and before long, the trembling becomes more and more violent as your body tries to, but can't, adjust for that loss of heat. That is the whole point of your body shaking and trembling; this movement is an involuntary muscle reflex produced by your body in an attempt to add warmth back to your system. Your body perspires when you run, or on a very hot day, in an attempt to help dispel built up body heat. On the other hand, if you are extremely cold or freezing and unable to move fast enough to generate the heat your body requires to keep going. At this point, your body starts to involuntary shiver and shake. While this explanation is not very technical, I think you get the picture.

During training, when a trainee started shaking uncontrollably, the old adage would usually come into play and the comment made, "He is shaking like a dog shitting peach seeds." Now mind you, I have never seen a dog shit peach seeds, but it sounds like a painful experience and one I am sure the dog would rather avoid. On the other hand, I have seen other men shivering from the cold, and I personally know the pain that accompanies losing so much body heat that you start to become hypothermic. If the dog is suffering as much as the man who is starting to freeze to death, then he can't be having much fun.

As I look back on BUDS, I can recall untold instances when we trainees were cold tested to our limit. Surprisingly enough, some of the coldest times that I can recall were spent at the Coronado Naval Amphibious Base swimming pool. The time spent in the cold water of the swimming pool couldn't compare to the time that we had to spend sitting on the pool deck, while other trainees were working with Instructors. Sitting on the cold pool deck was also a form of punishment, dealt at the hands of our Instructors, to those trainees who did something the Instructors did not approve of.

In Coronado, it seems that many of the mornings, when we were required to spend time at the pool, were overcast with a cold breeze blowing across the bay from San Diego or onshore from the Pacific Ocean. When we had completed whatever we were doing in the pool, we would be required to sit on a cold pool deck, with only a pair of UDT swim trunks to keep us warm. The problem came from the fact that we were wet and cold and not allowed to move around to replenish lost body heat. If we were forced to just sit there, then the worst thing that could possibly happen was inevitable. Our testicles would slowly move up into our stomach. Those two little scoundrels are smart enough to know that it is warmer in your stomach than lying there on the cold concrete pool deck, so they would inevitably make a hasty retreat and leave you to your misery. Now if you are a man that hasn't experienced this phenomenon, you should count yourself lucky. For those of you who know what I am talking about, take the pained expression off of your face and be thankful that you are not presently reliving that experience. For those of you who wonder what you do once this has happened, here it is. When this occurs, it becomes almost too painful to move, let alone stand up, but getting on your feet is something that, like it or not, you have to do. Once you have accomplished the difficult task of standing up, it is then necessary to stick your thumb into your groin cavity and, as painlessly as possible, remove your testicles one at a time. Trying to walk before you have removed your testicles produces excruciating pain, and it doesn't take but several steps before your mind and body won't let you go any farther. The first time you experience this is the most difficult and painful. Eventually, you become accustomed to this phenomenon, and it becomes easier; but believe me, it is never something you take for granted or look forward to.

Another cold testing incident that also happened during BUDS Training is one that makes me shiver even today. We were being taught the fine art of beach reconnaissance, but nothing Class-28 did that day would satisfy the Instructors' desire for perfection. We had started performing the actual reconnaissance during the early afternoon hours, but as the sun started to set, we had yet to satisfy the stringent requirements imposed by our Instructors.

For those of you who don't know, let me share some information about the nature of a beach reconnaissance and why it is performed. The primary purpose of a beach reconnaissance is to locate obstacles that have been placed in the ocean, primarily in the surf zone, to impede or destroy landing craft when they approach the beach. While the actual reconnaissance is difficult and somewhat complicated, the tools used to perform this task are really quite simple. Each swimmer is issued a plastic slate and pencil to write down any pertinent data found during the reconnaissance. The plastic slate is used because it is impervious to water, can be written on, and then later erased and used again. The second piece of gear is a lead line, or simply a fishing weight with a long piece of nylon cord or string attached. The cord has a single knot tied every one or two feet, two knots at ten feet, then single knots until you reach twenty feet where you find three knots and so on up to thirty feet where there are four knots. If the water is any deeper than this, you don't have to worry; the boat will easily clear almost any obstacle in water that deep.

At this point, the swimmers enter the water and maintain a straight line that extends from the beach out to sea. Ideally, this will be undertaken while maintaining roughly ten-foot intervals between swimmers. It is imperative that the line of swimmers remain perfectly straight, but this can become extremely difficult if the swimmers in the surf zone are being pummeled by waves.

In addition to the swimmers, there is a beach party that consists of four or more men. Two men hold light aluminum or bamboo poles eight to ten feet in length each with a bright colored flag or piece of cloth affixed to its top. These men line up one behind the other and hold each pole vertically to his body. The second man, or man in back, then aligns his pole directly behind the pole of the first man, and both men face the swimmers in the water. The men in the water then line up on the men holding the poles. You know that you are properly aligned when the two poles appear as one to each of the men in the water. Then, when given the signal, the poles are waved from side to side; each swimmer will first use his lead line to measure the depth of the water where he is positioned. The swimmers then search the water and the ocean floor, directly below and in their immediate area, for any obstacles that could possibly cause damage or impale a landing craft carrying assault troops. The swimmers then use their slate to record the depth of the water and any other pertinent information they have observed. While the swimmers are completing this task, another member, assigned to the beach party, will move down the beach to determine the sight of, and stage for, the next reading. The distance between readings could be ten to twenty feet but is usually determined by beach gradient and water visibility. It is also the responsibility of the beach party to provide cover fire, note any abnormalities related to this particular beach, and to identify permanent land fixtures that can later help guide assault boat coxswains delivering troops to the beach.

Beach surveys were first conducted during WWII, then Korea, and later during Vietnam. However, while the description just outlined will work well if you are reconnoitering a friendly beach it does not bode well if you are required to reconnoiter a beach controlled by the enemy. For hostile beaches, it would be impractical to have men standing on the beach waiving flags while being shot at and killed. Also, in a wartime situation, one of the primary objectives of reconnoitering a beach is to gather data without being observed by the enemy. Therefore, during BUDS and later in the Teams, you train and refine the tactics of beach reconnaissance until you have developed the discipline required to perform this activity without the help of a beach party, while under the pressure of varying and adverse conditions.

As I had mentioned earlier, Class-28 was going through the painful process of learning how to perform a beach reconnaissance, but not at all to the satisfaction of our BUDS Instructors. To add to our dilemma, the sun was now setting, we trainees were already cold, and it was about to get worse. Earlier in the afternoon, the Instructors had revoked the privilege of letting us wear our wet suit tops and the several hours spent in the ocean, without that protection, was starting to take its toll.

    We knew it was serious when the Instructors informed us that we would forgo dinner and continue working into the night and all night if that was deemed necessary. At that point, two trainees decided they had taken enough punishment and quit the program. For the next two hours, we worked harder than I thought possible but did eventually accomplish what the Instructors said they had been looking for all along. To this day, I don't honestly believe we were performing better. I think the Instructors had found what they were looking for all right and that had to do with the level of cold and suffering we were each willing to endure.

    We were now allowed to dress, but before we were marched back to our barracks, we were ordered to attention and marched into the ocean one last time. I think this reinforces what I mentioned earlier when I stated that the Instructors had an aversion to trainees in dry clothes. I can still remember marching back to our training area, each boat crew with their Inflatable Boat Small (IBS) balanced on their heads, and each man being so cold it didn't matter that the boat was bouncing up and down, trying to drive his neck down into his shoulders. When we passed the mess hall, on the way to our barracks, I didn't even care that we were not going to stop, all I could think about, and the only thing I wanted to do, was to stand under a hot shower and replenish some of the lost body heat. It was several hours, standing under the hot showers, and then wrapping myself in warm clothes and blankets before I fully recovered, but I did recover and no worse for wear.

Before graduating from BUDS and leaving the Teams, there would be other times that I would suffer from extreme cold. But this day and night, spent learning the fine art of beach reconnaissance, gave me the added assurance that I could handle these extreme conditions and recover from anything else that they wanted to throw my way. Yes, along with all of the other Class-28 trainees who endured that day, I had passed the test. I had been cold tested and survived.

12. YOU ARE WHAT YOU EAT

I have always liked the old saying, "You are what you eat." Before I joined the Navy and while I was in the Teams, it didn't make much difference what I ate, as long as there was plenty of it. When I would come home on leave, my grandmother and several of her friends from the altar society would pick me up and take me to this "all you can eat" restaurant south of Colorado Springs, my hometown. She just loved to see the plate pile up with chicken bones as she boasted to her friends, and anyone else who would listen, "If he tried hard enough, he could put this restaurant out of business."

Now, my grandmother knew a thing or two about cooking and eating. My grandparents owned a ranch north of Colorado Springs and east of the Air Force Academy, in an area called the Black Forest. They raised cattle, planted and harvested wheat, and processed lumber at their sawmill, which was situated not far from the ranch house. My grandmother cooked on a coal and wood-burning stove and at times would cook for her husband, two sons, and the mill hands. She was a very special woman, and this was quite an accomplishment, when compared to cooking on today's modern stoves and ranges. As far as my grandfather and nearly everyone else that she took care of were concerned, what she did for them and all that she was capable of doing was pretty much just taken for granted. Anyway, as we sat in that restaurant, my grandmother would tell her friends about the men at the ranch, and even though they could put away large quantities of food, no one could hold a candle to her grandson. I did love to eat, but I think a lot of this had to do with the fact that soaking wet, holding a five-pound weight, I weighed no more than one hundred-fifty pounds. It seemed that no matter how hard I tried, or how much I ate, I couldn't put on a pound. Needless to say, that changed as I grew older and my metabolism slowed down.

During Basic Underwater Demolition SEAL (BUDS) Training, we were certainly fed well and would even be given special access to the base mess hall during irregular hours. This was allowed to accommodate the uneven hours imposed by BUDS, as well as the strenuous demands of training and need for additional food intake to meet those demands. All in all, we were well taken care of and had few complaints about the quality or quantity of food available to us.

On the other end of the spectrum, when required to go on training maneuvers, away from Coronado, the routine of feeding trainees would take on a whole new dimension. During the time we spent at places like Camp Pendleton, practicing the fine art of beach reconnaissance or honing our skills related to sneak and peak operations, we would spend three to six days living on the beach with nothing to eat but C-rations. The government started preparing these meals during World War II as a replacement for the "Armored Rations" of World War I. Each of these meals came in a small cardboard box containing six cans. Three cans make up the main meal and consist of something like beans and wieners, scrambled eggs, stew or hash, plus vegetables. The three remaining cans consist of salted crackers, sugar, coffee and, if you were lucky, you just might get some sort of pound cake for dessert. The military started making both K and C-rations during World War II and continued to make and supply these rations throughout the Korean War and Vietnam. But, believe me, there is no way that K or C-rations could ever be mistaken for a gourmet meal. If anything, they were just tolerable.

During one of our training exercises at Camp Pendleton, some of the men started to complain of stomach problems after eating their C-rations. The Instructors assured the men that there was no problem with the food and that it was probably all in their minds. Several days passed when one of the trainees noticed a date on the box that contained the individual boxes of these rations that we had been eating. They were vintage World War II C-rations, manufactured in 1943, and, therefore, nearly twenty years old. When this was brought to the attention of the Instructors, we were again told not to worry because these meals were enclosed in tin cans; therefore, they would be perfectly good for many years to come. None of the Instructors ever complained of stomach problems, but why would they. They weren't eating the C-rations. They were eating freshly prepared meals from one of Camp Pendleton's mess halls. Complaints continued to fall on the deaf ears of our Instructors who remained steadfast in their assurance that there was nothing wrong with the rations.

    I should explain that during the early sixties, money was in short supply for the BUDS Training Unit as well as in the Teams. Therefore, a lot of scrounging was undertaken to get the very basics needed to operate, including the basic uniform worn by men in the Teams. This consisted of the basic green shirt and pants, supplied by the Army, and a standard soft cap that came from the Marine Corps. Because money was so scarce, every opportunity was taken to get whatever was needed for as little as possible, preferably for free. This didn't preclude taking from those that had when those that had weren't looking. I could, but won't go into that right now. Back to the World War II C-rations and how they ended up in the BUDS Training compound. It seems that when it came time to purchase the C-rations, a once in a lifetime opportunity presented itself. C-rations that had been produced more recently could be purchased for hard cash or, on the other hand, a large shipment of vintage WW II C-rations could be taken at no cost. Not wanting to look a gift horse in the mouth, it was decided that these older rations would do just fine, and the BUDS Training Unit became the proud recipient of a mountain of WW II C-rations. To belay any concerns we might have, one of the Instructors even told us a story about his little dog and how he had been eating the C-rations for nearly a year and had never complained. They fed; he ate, case closed. Therefore, if his dog could find nothing to complain about, then we trainees certainly had no right to complain.

Having concluded our training exercises at Pendleton, we returned to Coronado and welcomed eating once again at the Amphibious Base mess hall. With that, the stomach problems disappeared, and things were quickly back to normal. Then one evening as we staged for a night problem, we saw the little dog that belonged to our Instructor, the same dog that had been living on WW II C-rations for the past year. It was cold that evening and as the Instructor jumped out of his car, the little dog followed. When the Instructor stopped to talk to other Instructors, the small dog stood there shaking uncontrollably. He was a skinny little critter, and he had no hair. I mean he didn't have a single hair on his skinny little frame, and he was not one of those hairless dogs that I have seen but could never figure out. By the looks of him, I think this skinny little mutt would have been cold if he were standing in the sun on a hot day. It didn't take very long to figure out what had happened to this little dog and when asked, the Instructor said he and his wife couldn't figure out why the dog had started losing his hair when he started eating those WW II C-rations. We looked at each other, but concluded that we apparently hadn't eaten enough to make our hair fall out.

There were other instances when we were required to eat those C-rations and eat them we would. There would be more stomachaches and complaints, but when it came right down to it, we would eat the C-rations rather than go hungry. My hair was never adversely affected by eating those rations, but to this day, when I read, see, or hear, "you are what you eat," I look back on those magical days during Training when we ate the twenty year old, World War II, C-rations. I wonder if today's Training classes are still trying to finish them off, and I also can't help wondering about what happened to the hairless C-rat dog.

13. CLASS-28 VS. MARINES

It is not my desire to bring disparagement upon any branch of the military service, but it is a fact that there have always been problems when Navy and Marine Corps personnel are brought together. Any second year chemistry student can tell you that mixing Marine and Navy personnel will cause an explosion; it always does. This has been a fact since these two branches of the service were introduced to each other, and I am certain that it will continue until Congress abolishes one or both of them. It is, therefore, a certainty that this chemistry carries over to men from the Teams and Marine Corps personnel. Unfortunately, these issues were highlighted during WWII, when an issue was raised, vis-à-vis Marines claiming they were the first ashore when the U.S. Military assaulted an enemy-held beach. It seems that men from the Navy's Underwater Demolition Units (UDU's) took issue with this claim, made by the Marines, because they knew that UDU's were actually the first ashore. To enforce their position, men from UDU prepared a sign that read: "WELCOME U.S. MARINES, USO TWO BLOCKS TO THE LEFT" and placed this sign on the beach of a Japanese-held Island. They did this after they had cleared the surf zone and beach of enemy obstacles in preparation for the imminent Marine landing. As you can imagine, this wasn't received well by the Marines as they came ashore on D-day. From that day forward, the already unstable relationship between Marines and men from the Teams only worsened.

For Class-28, as well as other Basic Underwater Demolition Seal (BUDS) training classes of the sixties, the BUDS training barracks were not located in or near the Team Compound, on the Silver Strand, as they are today. They were situated at the far end of the Naval Amphibious Base, near the bay, directly across from San Diego. In fact, after you enter the

Amphibious Base, if you were to continue driving straight until you reached the bay and then turned left about two hundred yards, that is where the training barracks were located at that time. Being this near the bay made it easy for the Instructors to dole out punishment to trainees, which usually required that the trainees spend time in the cold water of the bay. Also, this proximity to the bay meant that we trainees didn't have far to go to get wet, and wet we were most of the time. Wet and cold was a way of life during training and if a man had a problem with this fact, then it was unlikely that he would complete BUDS.

Now, directly behind our barracks just happened to be the barracks that housed transient Marines who came to Coronado from Pendleton to train in the fine art of Amphibious Landings. Their training consisted of learning how to scale cargo nets and exit an amphibious landing craft, as well as assaulting a beach, after that beach had been cleared of obstacles by men from the Teams of course. We had little time to socialize, but on occasion BUDS trainees and Marines would clash; words would be exchanged and fists would fly. I don't recall a trainee ever losing one of those fights, and this didn't sit too well with the officer in charge of the Marine detachment.

It was about the eighth week of training when two trainees clashed with five Marines and literally hung them out to dry. The BUDS Instructors heard what had happened and didn't have a problem with it until a Marine Major caught up with our class and BUDS Instructors, just outside of the Amphibious Base swimming pool. He drove up screaming about the butt kicking his five men had been handed and wanted the two BUDS trainees who had done the dastardly deed punished. Several Instructors patiently listened to the Officer, and we also stood nearby, listened, and smirked as he carried on. Then, out of the clear blue, one of the trainees started singing a song BUDS classes sing to keep their minds off of the pain endured during training. Then, in unison, the entire class joined in. The song was the UDT/SEAL version of the Marine Corp fight song and, in part, went something like this: "From the halls of Montezuma to the Shores of Tripoli, all the jobs to tough for leather necks are done by UDT." Well, that should give you some idea of what was to come because this song is very near and dear to the hearts of all Marines, including the Marine Major who by now was livid.

At this point, the Marine ordered the BUDS Instructors to punish Class-28 for singing a song that denigrated the Marine Corp. By now, he had forgotten what he had originally intended to accomplish and had lost what little composure he had left. This man was certainly not displaying the attributes befitting a Marine Officer. With that, one of the BUDS Instructors explained to the Major that he was appalled at what he had just heard and screamed an order for Class-28 to assume the position and start doing push-ups. We immediately dropped and started counting out push-ups, push-ups that I knew would continue all day. Then the Instructor did something I will never forget. He shouted, "I told you to do push-ups; I didn't tell you to stop singing." So with that, we did push-ups and sang Marine Corps related songs for the Major, which included another that stated: "Oh leather neck, on bended knee, can kiss the ass of UDT." As you can imagine, by this time the Major was far beyond livid, he was beside himself, but he could do nothing more than scream, "You haven't heard the end of this." His final words, as he was driving away, were something to the effect that he would have our collective behinds and that this confrontation was far from over. With that, he left. The Instructors ordered us to recover from the push-up position, and they then marched a triumphant Class-28 into the swimming pool area. It was at times like this that I knew I was where I belonged, and it was because of times like this that I gained an even deeper respect for our BUDS Instructors.

A week passed before we were once again reminded about our visit from the Marine Major. One night, as we were returning from a night problem, we approached a group of Marines who were clustered outside of our training barracks. Apparently, the Marine Major had gathered his men, when he was unable to gain sympathy from the senior BUDS Training Officer or the Naval Amphibious Base Commanding Officer, and told them they would have to defend the honor of the Marine Corps because of what had happened. They were there to kick our butts and teach us that it wasn't wise to sing songs that dishonored their beloved Corps. Now, before I go any further, it is important to insert a fact that BUDS trainees learn in one of the early phases of training. Simply stated by a BUDS Instructor: "While you may not be the toughest men in the world, you will be among the best conditioned. In a fight, though you may be knocked down time and again, because of this conditioning and your desire to win at any cost, you will be able to regain your feet each time. Eventually, when your adversary can no longer muster the strength to knock you down again, you will simply kick his ass." When the smoke finally cleared, a lesson had been learned all right, but not by the BUDS trainees, rather a lesson had been learned by the Marines. That day, they learned that it wasn't wise to call out BUDS trainees and that the wisest thing they could have done would have been to walk away. This turned out to be a bitter defeat for the Marines and would only serve to kindle a fire in the BUDS trainees. This fire would soon move the BUDS trainees to conjure up more innovative ways to punish those men, who unfortunately occupied the barracks, directly behind the BUDS training barracks.

14. LACK OF SLEEP AND BOOBY-TRAPS

During Basic Underwater Demolition SEAL Training (BUDS), we soon found that sleep was a luxury not to be taken lightly. There were weekly, and often twice weekly, night problems, mandated throughout training that would eat away at the hours normally spent sleeping. Occasionally, these problems lasted all night. During Hell Week, we were not afforded the luxury of sleep. Then, during the final three weeks of training spent at San Clemente Island, sleep became an even greater luxury. Failed problems by the trainees would have to be repeated until done correctly. This would occupy the late night hours normally spent sleeping. As more and more problems were repeated, twenty-four hour days became the norm, and the class was again denied the luxury of sleep for long periods of time. It was the wise man who took advantage of the minutes not occupied by the demands of training or the Instructors and tried to catch up on lost and much needed sleep.

During the final phase of training at San Clemente, there was another danger that awaited the exhausted and overworked trainee when he returned from a night problem, "Booby Traps." There were no permanent structures at our San Clemente Base Camp, so our quarters were comprised of large Army tents; each tent could accommodate eight to ten men. There was no electricity, so each tent had one lantern to provide the only source of light. However, most of the time, we were not allowed to use the lantern because it was another luxury that the Instructors felt we had not earned. Therefore, it became a matter of feeling around in the darkness to locate personal belongings and the cot to which we had been assigned. It was in this darkness and uncertainty that the booby traps came into play.

Late one night, upon returning from a repeated problem, we were exhausted and ill prepared for the reception we were about to receive. While we had been away from our compound, the Instructors had placed booby-traps in each of the trainee tents. They were small devices called "Matchbox" and "Mousetrap" booby-traps. Small though they were, they were quite capable of causing damage to an appendage if you were close enough to the device when it detonated.

These two types of booby-traps received their names because of their size and shape. One is quite similar to a small matchbox, and the other a small box with a spring that operates a door. Each device comes with a small blasting cap attached to its body, which is used to detonate a larger explosive charge. The matchbox is attached to a trip wire. Stepping on or stumbling into that trip wire causes the two pieces of the matchbox to separate and the device to explode. On the other hand, a mousetrap is a small box-like device that has a door that is activated by a spring. To set the device, you simply close the door and place it under an object. That object could be any number of items such as a pillow, book, clothing, equipment, etc. The weight of the object, even a very light weight, will hold the door shut and prevent the device from detonating. However, picking up or moving the object placed over the device will cause the door to spring open and the booby-trap to detonate. You may also use a trip wire to detonate this type of booby-trap.

Luckily for us, it was never the intent of the Instructors to permanently maim or kill a trainee. Therefore, they only used the small blasting cap when booby-trapping our tents. Don't get me wrong, if not careful, a trainee could easily lose an eye or suffer burns or lacerations if exposed skin were too close to the device when it detonated.

This first night, the Instructors placed the booby traps several inches off the floor in the trainee tents and used trip wire to detonate them. Most were placed near the entrance, and most were detonated by the first person entering the tent. This was done to let the trainees know that other devices could be hidden throughout the tent and that a thorough search would be required before anyone could even think about sleep. The Instructors had forbidden us from using our lanterns; thus, the long and slow process, probing by hand for the booby-traps, would be required. It would take us better than an hour to complete this task and only then as the sun was starting to come up.

Our first exposure to booby-traps occurred earlier in training, long before we arrived at San Clemente. Our Instructors would use them during classroom instruction. When given a brake, the Instructors would place these devices between desks, using a trip wire. They would also put the mousetrap devices in our notebooks, set to explode when we opened them after the break. It didn't take long before we became very aware of our surroundings and any changes that may have transpired during our absence. You could never tell when you might have been set-up by the Instructors. Having one of these devices go off in a trainee's notebook would usually destroy all the information that it contained, causing him to assimilate the data he had lost from scratch.

I can recall one instance where a trainee, who kept nodding off during a classroom training session, was given a live hand grenade. When he had a good grip on the grenade, the Instructor pulled the pin and informed him that it was all right if he wanted to go back to sleep. I don't have to tell you that this was the most wide-awake trainee for the balance of that session. Needless to say, the trainees around him kept a close eye on him as well. Then, when the session had ended and the Instructor reinserted the pin, it took two trainees to pry his fingers loose from the grenade.

Booby-traps, that first night at San Clemente, had caught us off guard. But, I can assure you that wouldn't happen again. On future nights, we would find the mousetrap devices that had been placed under our pillows or in and under our duffle bags, where our gear was stowed. We would find the matchbox devices, strung with trip wire, across our bunks. Quite often, these mandatory searches would prevent us from getting any sleep, but each trainee would carry a valuable lesson into the Teams. Sleep is a passing luxury that can be made up at another time. Tripping a booby-trap can cause death, and death is permanent, never to be made up.

15. BLOWING THINGS UP

During my time in the Teams, I would be given my share of assignments involving explosives. Each quarter, every man in the Teams is required to qualify for double hazardous duty pay in two of three specialties. They are diving, demolitions, and parachuting. The third was added in the early 1960's, as more and more men became jump qualified. You could not receive triple hazardous pay, even though most men in the Teams remained qualified in all three disciplines. Demolitions was my favorite of the three specialties, and I always looked forward to blowing things up.

My fascination with explosives started during training. At this time, we were provided ample opportunity to learn both the negative and positive aspects of various types of explosives. Our work with explosives started shortly after Hell Week, but it wasn't until we went to San Clemente that we received real hands-on experience with large shots. During this final phase of training, there were two incidents related to explosives that remain as fresh in my memory today as the day they happened.

For me, the most difficult period of BUDS Training had to be the three final weeks of training, spent at San Clemente Island. And of those three weeks, the single most difficult day was one spent loading obstacles. The obstacles I refer to are similar to the ones that awaited the WW II Allied Forces coming ashore during the D-day invasion at Normandy. For the men of the Teams, called Naval Combat Demolition Units (NCDU) at that time, their most important job would be destroying those obstacles before the commencement of D-Day landings.

There are numerous and varying types of obstacles, but the one I will be referring to is called the German or Japanese Scully. This is a three-foot square block of concrete that stands roughly three-feet high. Imbedded in the concrete are two spikes, made from railroad track, that stick another three feet above its top. During fabrication and before the concrete hardens, the two lengths of railroad track are placed deep into the concrete at a slight angle. When thoroughly cured, the obstacle is placed off of the beach, in the surf zone, in approximately seven to nine feet of water. The spikes face seaward toward oncoming boats. Then, when a landing craft carrying troops approaches the beach, it becomes impelled on the spikes. The men in the boat become easy targets, or drown, as they exit the boat to go ashore. In addition, these obstacles can easily be booby-trapped. When this is done, the landing craft explodes on contact with the obstacle, blowing the bottom out of the craft and killing the men on board.

During BUDS, it is imperative for each trainee to become thoroughly familiar with explosives and learn how to destroy obstacles as well as various other potential targets. Destroying an obstacle isn't as simple as swimming in, attaching explosives, pulling the fuse, and returning to the waiting pick-up boat for recovery. It is in fact much more complicated than that. Multiple obstacles require that you run a trunk line between each so they can all be blown at one time. This prevents individual shots from going off, killing any swimmer still in the area. Also, to properly destroy an underwater obstacle of this type, you must place the explosives on its seaward side. The explosives must then be secured as tightly to the obstacle as possible; this is the most important aspect of blowing something up. Attaching explosives to an obstacle is accomplished by using rope that comes in the haversack, or satchel containing the explosives. If done properly, the obstacle will either be completely destroyed, or blown up onto the beach where it will no longer present a hazard to incoming boats. Properly loading obstacles requires close team work that is very labor intensive.

We had our first taste of loading obstacles shortly after Hell Week, of all places, in the Coronado Amphibious Base swimming pool. They were mock obstacles, made of three-quarter inch steel bars, welded together, and covered with aluminum. They were then placed in the pool, and we would swim down and practice tying the explosives to the obstacle, as tightly as possible, or at least tightly enough to satisfy the Instructors. That, however, wasn't possible. We would place the explosives, and the Instructors would pull them free. We would then replace the explosives, this time tying them so tightly that the aluminum and steel bars would bend. Still, the Instructors would pull them loose and then express their dissatisfaction with our poor performance. The lesson they were trying to teach us was that no matter how tightly the explosives were tied to the obstacle, it wasn't tight enough, so make it tighter. The Instructors would become even more demanding when we went to work loading and destroying the real obstacles at San Clemente.

At San Clemente, we were required to complete a morning, noon, and night problem. In addition, each problem must meet the strict guidelines imposed by our Instructors. Failing to do so meant repeating the problem, causing future problems to slip into the late night or early morning hours. We soon found that it wasn't possible to complete a problem to the satisfaction of the Instructors and before long, we were working around the clock trying to catch up, but never quite doing so. This soon became three weeks of hell, and each week tougher than Hell Week.

Soon after we arrived at San Clemente, our entire class was ordered to muster at a lagoon located several hundred yards from the tents we called home. It was early afternoon, and our first problem would be that of loading obstacles. The water in the lagoon was calm but extremely cold. The obstacles were placed in about twenty feet of water, much deeper than they would be placed in a real combat situation. At this depth, the distance between the boat's bottom and the impelling spikes of the obstacle would have been far too great to cause any concern. The obstacles had been placed at this depth for one reason, to make it more difficult for the trainee. To load the obstacle, we would free dive, no diving gear allowed. This meant that the longer you could hold your breath the better. We worked in teams of two, and each member of the team would be required to descend a number of times in order to successfully load an obstacle.

We paired up, entered the water, and started to work. My swim partner was Jim Foley, a strong swimmer, hard worker, and solid performer. We worked well together and, after several dives each, called the Instructor to check our work. The Instructor pulled the haversack from the obstacle and returned to the surface screaming at us for taking too long to do a second-rate job. He went on to say that it took too many dives, and the quality was substandard at best. He then said that our wet-suit tops apparently made us too buoyant, and he knew the perfect solution to our problem.

During training, you must earn the privilege to wear a wet-suit top. That happens after Hell Week, but not until you have earned your swim fins. You are required to make long ocean swims, without the protection of a wet-suit top, before the Instructors feel you have earned the right to such a luxury. Then when you finally make that first swim in your new top, it's like receiving a reprieve from hell. I said wet-suit top because you are not fitted for wet-suit bottoms until you complete training and enter the Teams. In addition, during training the privilege of wearing the protective top can be revoked at any time by the Instructors. And believe me; this happened more often than not.

Because we had failed so miserably during our first attempt at loading the obstacle, the Instructor ordered us to remove our wet-suit tops. He said that the top obviously prevented us from spending enough quality time with the obstacle and that he was certain we would do much better without it. This was not what we had wanted to hear, but we did as ordered. We then went back into the water and to work. Soon, we could see other teammates removing their tops until, finally, the entire class was without the comfort of a wet suit.

Again and again, we dove into the freezing water to attach the haversack to the obstacle, only to have the Instructor tear it loose and order us to start over. One hour turned quickly into two and then three. Hypothermia was now starting to make it more and more difficult to perform. Both Jim and I were shaking uncontrollably, and the time we were able to stay underwater grew shorter with each dive. Holding our breath, for any length of time, grew to be an almost insurmountable hurdle to overcome. We continued for another two hours but at this point, neither Jim nor I could think, let alone work underwater. We were played out, but we continued to dive and do the best we could.

Then, after five hours, the Instructors ordered us out of the water. According to them, we had failed miserably and would have to repeat this problem the following day. At this point, we were just happy to leave the freezing water and put on some warn clothes. Then that evening, when we attempted and failed the night problem, we found ourselves with two problems completed and two problems to be repeated. Both would have to be made up, and we had only finished our first full day on the Island. And so it would go for the next three weeks.

While at San Clemente, we would never complete a problem, on our first attempt, to the satisfaction of the Instructors. Though we didn't know it at the time that is how it was intended to be. As far as loading obstacles, we would come back the next day to successfully resolve the previous day's problems. On this day, we would not only set the explosives, we would destroy the obstacles as well. Apparently, all of the Instructors' abuse and rejection had paid off; each of the obstacles was successfully destroyed or blown up onto the beach and out of harm's way. Most importantly, we had learned a lesson: When destroying an obstacle, you can never affix the explosives too tightly. And though this may seem like a simple lesson, it would serve us well when we graduated to the Teams.

The second incident occurred one night, during our second week at San Clemente. A detachment of Navy See Bees had come to the Island to conduct training exercises. They had established their base camp at the top of a cliff, about a half-mile from our compound, high above the ocean. We could see them, but we had no interface with them and really didn't know or care what they were doing, or why they were there.

We had just completed our afternoon problem, finished dinner, and were now waiting for the Instructors to brief us on the forthcoming night problem. Though we didn't know it at the time, this would prove to be one of the only fun problems we would undertake during our three weeks on the Island.

When called together for our nightly briefing, we were told that our problem that night involved the See Bees. We were to load several hundred pounds of explosives on the side of the cliff, below where the See Bees were camped. We would then set a time fuse, escape to our boats at the base of the cliff, and paddle out into the bay to watch the fireworks. This would be a true test, involving much of what we had learned in training. We would have to employ previously taught stealth techniques, when climbing the cliff near their camp, to avoid being spotted by the See Bees patrolling the perimeter of their camp. We would then set the explosives to control the blast so we didn't hurt or kill any of the men camped out on top of the cliff. If we could pull this off without being spotted, it would prove that we were ready to graduate to the Teams. Or at least this is how we trainees perceived it.

At this point, we went to work preparing the explosives and peripheral components needed to accomplish this mission. We then readied our boats and prepared ourselves for the operation. Each boat crew was assigned duties they would be accountable for. Then we went over the operation again and again until every man understood what his responsibilities entailed. When the Instructors felt we were ready, they told us to go to our boats and wait until they signaled it was time to move out.

At zero two hundred hours, or two a.m., we were given the go ahead and entered the water. We would paddle to the cliff below the See Bee camp. The men with the explosives would climb the shear cliff and place them. Another team of men would scale the cliff to observe the See Bee sentries and deal with them if the operation were jeopardized. It wouldn't be our objective to physically harm these men; we were just carrying out the problem as though we were in a real combat situation. An Instructor accompanied the men who were to place the explosives and light the fuse, which would detonate the explosives. He was there to grade our overall performance and make certain that everything we did was safe and correct. Other boat crews would paddle the remaining boats offshore and wait until the explosive handlers and their security force had returned to the beach. They would then paddle in with their boats for the extraction.

It took less than an hour to secure the area, set the explosives, and return to the waiting boats. The Instructor and trainee who stayed behind to light the fuse were the last to return. In addition, two Instructors stayed at the top of the cliff, away from the explosives, and out of sight of the See Bee sentries. They were there to stop anyone from accidentally wandering near or stumbling onto the explosives and being killed.

      We paddled our boats to a safe distance offshore and waited. What would then happen will forever remain a picture in my mind. There was a tremendous flash of light that turned night into day. Then followed an ear deafening, thunderous explosion and the accompanying concussion. The sight was something to behold and as we sat there motionless, transfixed on all that we were seeing, the See Bees were reacting differently. Tents were being knocked to the ground, men were running in circles, others were bumping into each other, and some were falling down, each man totally disoriented. And all the while, it was as though this were happening in slow motion. There was one certainty, these men had been given a new outlook on life, and I would bet they would not soon forget this night. It would take a while for the grip of lost darkness to once again take hold. Then, when it did, we paddled our boats back to the compound. And, though the Instructors wouldn't admit it, Class-28 had pulled it off and passed a critical test. We would soon be ready for our place in the Teams.

Nick Nickelson at San Clemente Island during explosives training.

16. A CRITICAL SITUATION

We were into our third week at San Clemente Island and making preparations for a night problem that we anxiously anticipated. This may have been the only problem, while at Clemente, or during training for that matter, that the trainees of Class-28 actually looked forward to. For this particular night problem, each boat crew would be given a map, a compass, and a set of map coordinates. This night was intended to prove or disprove our navigational capabilities. Each boat crew would follow the prescribed coordinates to the other side of the Island and locate an item, previously sealed inside a tin can and buried by the instructors. These items had been buried in separate and varied locations, so each boat crew would be given a different set of map coordinates before being sent on its way.

For this exercise we would be on our own, working within our individual boat crews, without Instructors breathing down our necks. While we relished the fact that we would be operating without Instructors, the most important aspect of this night problem was the fact that it did not involve water; therefore we would be in warm clothes and dry. There were very few times during BUDS when we were not wet and cold so we planned to make the most of this unusual opportunity.

It was roughly twenty hundred hours or eight at night when we started. We were told that the round trip, if we ran and jogged, and we were expected to run and jog, would take no more than four to five hours. Therefore we should have no problem locating our target and returning to our base camp by no later than zero one hundred hours or one in the morning. Whenever the Instructors used the word "should" you knew they actually meant, "would" and that punishment awaited those boat crews who didn't adhere to this deadline.

At this point of training, all of the men assigned to the boat crew, to which I was assigned, had been together since shortly after "Hell Week". We therefore knew each other well and had a good understanding of each other's strengths and capabilities. I purposely didn't say strengths and weaknesses because those men who reached this point of training did not possess weaknesses or at least weaknesses worth mentioning.

Our boat crew consisted of five men, two of which were officers. This was unusual because a normal boat crew would be comprised of one officer and six enlisted men. However, due to attrition, the standard Class-28 boat crew consisted of one officer and four enlisted men. The officer serves as the boat coxswain and it is his job to sit in the aft section of the Inflatable Boat Small (IBS) and steer the boat. The remaining four men are stationed two on each side of the IBS and it is their job to paddle. As I mentioned earlier, due to heavy attrition, Class-28 had nine boat crews and ten officers. Therefore, our boat crew wound up with two officers and they were both solid operators as well as excellent officers.

Mike Paul was our boat coxswain and a real character. He is also a man I have included in numerous other stories so I won't elaborate. Peter Riddle (Pete) was the second officer assigned to our boat crew. Pete was the tallest member of our class, standing at least six foot six inches. He was also a person who possessed that rare ability of being funny without attempting to do so or even knowing that he was being funny. It would be Mr. Riddle and some of his impromptu comments that kept our boat crew laughing when times were really difficult. Tony Zimos, Larry Miller and yours truly made up the balance of the boat crew and in time we became a well-oiled machine and excelled in all matters related to operating as a boat crew during BUDS training.

San Clemente Island, where we conducted our final three weeks of training, is the southernmost of the eight Channel Islands, situated in the Pacific Ocean, off the coast of Southern California. It is roughly twenty miles long, five miles wide, and is comprised of some very steep mountains and difficult terrain. I always thought San Clement was the sister Island of Santa Catalina because they are relatively near each other. However, unlike Catalina which is visible from all Los Angeles coastal cities, San Clemente is much further from the coast and not readily visible. In addition, unlike Santa Catalina, the Island of San Clemente is owned by the United States Government and has served as a Naval training site and target range since 1934.

Now, back to our night problem. It was due to the steep gradient and difficult terrain of San Clemente Island that we would be afforded four to five hours to complete a problem that only required that we traverse a five-mile stretch to the appointed target, then a five mile return trip to our base camp. As the crow flies this would not have proven to be a difficult task but because we aren't crows, we would be required to traverse a number of the steep hills that make up San Clemente Island, then do the same on the return leg of this particular night problem.

Roughly half way through the first leg of our trip, Pete's humor came into play. Though he didn't know it at the time he was about to put forth one of his all time greats. We were crossing a field and in the darkness it was difficult to see the ground under our feet let alone where we were placing each foot as we jogged along to our designated target. As we were charging forward I heard a low groan from Mr. Riddle and he then came to an abrupt halt. Pete looked like a man who had just stepped on a land mine. He stood there frozen not willing to take a step in any direction for fear it might detonate. He then said, "Nickelson, you have to help me, something has attached itself to my leg and won't let go." By this time he had pulled out his K-bar knife and was making futile gestures toward his ankle trying to dislodge whatever evil creature had taken hold of his leg just above the top of his boot. As I walked back it happened, Mr. Riddle then said, "Nickelson, this is a critical situation, be very careful that it doesn't attack you." By now the other three members of our boat crew had returned to where Pete and I were standing but they were warned to hold their ground and come no closer. As I approached he just stood there and repeated, "Nickelson, what we have here is a critical situation." I must admit I was very cautious as I moved forward with my K-bar knife drawn and ready, prepared to kill this varmint that had attached itself to Pete's leg and was most assuredly sucking his blood. Then, as I reached down and pulled-up his pant's leg what I found attached to Mr. Riddle's sock was a very large bur, or prickly seed capsule from one of San Clemente's native plants, not the creature we had anticipated finding. We were all relieved that it was not the blood-sucking critter that we had expected to find and as I removed it, Mr. Riddle heaved a huge sigh of relief. I started to laugh and it was all I could do to regain my feet as I thought about Mr. Riddle's repeated statement; "Nickelson, this is a critical situation." The other members of our boat crew thought it was equally funny and after a few minutes even Pete started to laugh. This was simply an example of Mr. Riddle being able to lighten-up a difficult situation without intending to or even knowing that he had done so.

As for the operation at hand, we would go on to find the item, buried by the Instructors, and return to our base camp within the allotted time given to complete this particular night problem. As for Mr. Riddle, he would continue to say things that would lighten up almost any difficult situation and for that I would always hold him in fond esteem.

Soon after the conclusion of this particular night problem, training for Class-28 would come to an end and we would receive the new assignments we had worked so hard to attain. We would be awarded our individual places in the Teams. Then, like every man who had gone before us, we would find ourselves embroiled in life threatening and truly critical situations. Whenever this would happen, if given the time and under certain conditions, I would think back on that night at San Clemente and the comment made by Mr. Riddle; "Nickelson, this is a critical situation" and somehow the thought of that night and those few words would help relieve the tension of the current situation and make it seem just a little less overwhelming.

Left to right: Larry Miller, Mr. Pete Riddle, Tony Zimos, and Mr. Mike Paul. These were the other four members that made up the boat crew to which I was assigned.

17. THE SWIM THAT DIDN'T HAPPEN

As I previously mentioned, the final three weeks of BUDS Training are spent at San Clemente, an Island in the Pacific Ocean one hundred Kilometers north west of San Diego. The Island, controlled by the Navy, is isolated and, therefore, a perfect location for pulling together all that had been previously taught in BUDS. Civilians are prohibited and the only living creatures I can remember seeing on the Island were wild goats. This was a place where Naval Air practiced live bomb runs and where we were able to fire weapons, use all types of explosives, blow obstacles, and literally raise hell without worrying about killing someone other than ourselves.

Now, most people think the hardest part of training is Hell Week, but they are sadly mistaken. San Clemente is Hell times Three Weeks. During this final phase of training, you are given three problems a day, and each must be successfully completed in a prescribed time frame as determined by the Instructors. Problems consist of loading and blowing obstacles, sneak and peek operations, land navigation, long ocean swims across kelp beds, and the list goes on and on. Now if you fail to complete, say the morning problem, to the Instructor's satisfaction, then you must repeat that problem in the afternoon. That then pushes the afternoon problem to night and the night to late night and so on and so on. Although you don't know it at the time, it is literally impossible to finish a problem to the instructor's satisfaction, but that is the way they had planned it. By day two, we were backed up and by week two, we were doing problems one after another twenty-four hours a day, seven days a week, and we were still unable to catch up. This is not unlike Hell Week, except for the fact that Hell Week lasted only one week.

By the end of the second week, everyone was exhausted. Even this near the completion of training, men were still quitting the program. Hard as that was to imagine, some just couldn't take any more, and that was what the Instructors had intended to find out. To quit now is one thing, but to quit in combat could cost lives and that is unacceptable.

One night, toward the end of week three, we were ordered to report to a beach that was located near our compound. It was raining, windy and cold, a truly miserable night for trainees but one made to order for the Instructors. We had been staging for a makeup problem, so we wondered why the sudden change. One of the Instructors ordered us to form a straight line and to remove all of our clothing. We looked at each other and did what we were ordered to do. The Instructor then said he would return shortly, ordered us to stand at attention, and left. Ten, then fifteen minutes went by, still no Instructor and by this time, we were all freezing. Finally, after twenty minutes, two Instructors returned and told us that there had been a change in plans.

For several minutes, the Instructors paraded around forty half-frozen trainees and then ordered us to swim naked around a small island that rests in the water, about a half-mile offshore. It wasn't really an Island, but rather a large rock and a prominent landmark of San Clemente, commonly referred to as "Bird Shit Rock." The rock is inhabited by birds and the bird droppings, over time, have turned it white, thus giving it the name. Now, try to imagine forty men, shivering and trying to comprehend what had been ordered. Some actually broke down and cried, two decided they had endured enough and quit the program, and the rest awaited the order to proceed.

In an exercise of this nature, the Instructor translates orders by means of a whistle. One blast from the whistle means go, two means stop, and three means return to the beach. We stood in disbelief as we heard the shrill sound of the whistle. Could this really be happening? Then, once again, a single blast from the whistle and the Instructor shouting, "What are you waiting for, ladies?" We knew now that it was for real, and we all started moving toward the water and the mile swim. When everyone was in the water, we heard two blasts from the whistle and stopped, all of us treading water and waiting for the single blast, which would mean we were to start again. What we heard next was one the sweetest sounds I can remember hearing during those three weeks at San Clemente, three blasts from the whistle. That meant for us to return to the beach, could it be, and then three blasts once more. We returned, not knowing what would happen next. Would the Instructors line us up again and send us back into the water? Just what the plan was, we simply didn't know.

The Instructors then told us we had two minutes to get dressed and said if we took one second longer, we would complete the swim in our clothes. Now dressed and still wondering what was happening, we were told by the Instructors to assemble in front of a wooden-framed structure covered by a tent that was used as our mess hall. We were ordered to stand there, at attention, as the Instructors walked around back. Suddenly, the door swung open and as our eyes adjusted to the light, spread out before us was a meal fit for a king. We were then ordered to enter and enjoy. In utter disbelief we stood there. This was unlike anything that had happened to us during training, and we weren't sure what to do. We soon found out that the gesture was real, and we went in and enjoyed one of the best and most appreciated meals that I have ever eaten. We had passed yet another test; yes we would have made the swim; the Instructors didn't question that. This reward was given, not for passing this test alone, but for passing all the other tests given throughout training.

During training, when a person quits the program, he is immediately distanced from other classmates, never to be seen again. He is then reassigned to the regular Navy and another fleet assignment. Now, as I sat in the warm mess hall, I couldn't help but think about the two men who had dropped out of training only hours earlier. I wondered what they would have thought had they known that they would forever be remembered for refusing to make "The swim that didn't happen." As for BUDS Class-28, my class, we would soon complete training and take our place in the Teams.

Some time later, R.D. Russell, a friend and graduate of BUDS Class-29, stated that while concluding their training at San Clemente Island, his class had been placed in the same quandary, regarding the swim, as was Class-28. Class-29 marched to the waters edge and, like Class-28, they were recalled at the last moment and fed a great meal. Then, someone in the next class, Class-30, found out what had happened to Classes-28/29 and prepared his classmates for what was to come. They entered the water knowing they would soon hear three blasts from the whistle, return to the beach, and reap the reward of a hot meal that awaited them. However, for Class-30 there was a problem; their logic was flawed. The Instructors knew that the students had been informed about what had happened with Classes 28 and 29, so guess what? Right, no three blasts on the whistle, Class-30 did make the swim around "Bird Shit Rock." The lesson for future trainees, don't try to second-guess what awaits you in training; you will always be wrong. Most importantly, don't try to second-guess the Instructors; they will always surprise you.

GOOD TIMES IN THE TEAMS:

Nick Nickelson surrounded by weapons, equipment, and explosives each Team member is qualified to use.

Nick Nickelson six months after joining UDT-12. Food was good but the weight training was even better.

18. THE OLD OAK TREE

As I made my way into the Teams I was awestruck when I first met and talked to the men who had spent many long years in the Teams before I arrived. These men were the lifers or old timers as they were more affectionately referred to and they had been where the action was and therefore possessed all of the answers. These were also the men who wouldn't have given us the time of day only a month earlier and now they were there to answer questions and indoctrinate us in all maters related to the Teams. By graduating from BUDS Training we had earned their acceptance but we still had much to learn and they would be the ones who would teach us.

One of the finest men that I met when I crossed the road that separated BUDS Training from the Team Compound was Bill Corey, a Chief Petty Officer. Bill was second in command of the Platoon to which I was assigned and he was an old salt. By "old salt" I mean that he was a lifer, a career Navy man, a man who had been in the Navy for a long time and had seen it all. Bill was a Chief Boatswains Mate and if you are unfamiliar with the Navy's system of rating and ranking enlisted personnel, the Chief Boatswains Mate is at the top of the food chain for enlisted personnel. Also, to reach the rank of Chief Boatswains Mate, one has most assuredly done so by fighting his way from the rank of a lowly seaman, the junior rank of Navy enlisted personnel, to this coveted position. In addition, the Chief Boatswains Mate must know every aspect of shipboard life as well as how to run a ship. Basically, he knows where every bone is buried. The Chief Boatswains Mate knows how to read and work enlisted personnel, even the most incorrigible, and is the one enlisted man aboard ship most trusted by the Captain. Although we were in the Teams, not aboard ship, this trust between the Team Captain and his Chief Boatswains Mate was still firmly entrenched.

More than any other man in Teams, I enjoyed every minute I spent with Chief Corey. He was a teacher par-excellence and was always there when called upon. He was not a man who took trust lightly and in order to be accepted by Chief Corey you had to earn his trust and that came at the price of hard work, honesty, and giving one hundred percent to every task, assignment, or operation you were entrusted to carry out. Bill was pure Navy and that was born out one day when he told me that the Navy was first and foremost in his life and came even before his family.

Chief Corey, as well as other senior enlisted men we were to learn from, taught from experience. The many lessons these men had learned, the hard way, would be passed on to us, the new arrivals. This would be no easy matter because, of the thirty-five enlisted men who graduated from BUDS Class-28, twenty-two had been assigned to training straight out of boot camp and therefore had no prior Naval experience. Although young and inexperienced, these men shared one thing in common, an eagerness to learn from the best and learn they would.

The importance of learning from those who had gone before and paid their dues was emphasized in a sign that was permanently posted in the UDT/SEAL Team Briefing Room. I was significantly and permanently impacted by this sign and it is as important in my life today as it was then, nearly forty years ago. The sign simply stated; "You must learn from the mistakes of others, in the Teams you will not live long enough to make them all yourself." It literally meant that we would be the protégé's of men who had witnessed the costly mistakes of others or had made serious mistakes and survived. Nonetheless, it meant that we were to heed well the lessons these senior Team members were to teach us.

The lessons we were to learn not only came from hands on experience but from stories. I truly enjoyed listening to Chief Corey and other senior Team members reminisce about past experiences and operations they had undertaken during the years before we arrived. For me, it was a wonderful learning experience. It is true that I had read about some of the operations attributed to Naval Special Warfare but prior to the early sixties there were few books that adequately documented the exploits of the Teams. Therefore, from the stories told to us we would learn as surely as we would learn from those lessons taught during actual operations. There was an incident that had occurred several years before my arrival and though it is not one that conjures up positive mental pictures of Team bravado, it was nonetheless an interesting story.

In training as well as in the Teams we learned the intricacies of numerous types of explosives and experimented with various ways of removing obstacles both in the water and on land. Each member of the UDT/SEAL Teams is an expert in explosives and is well trained in all aspects of this fine art. As the story goes, a Team member, and I won't mention his name except to say it wasn't Chief Corey, was at his home one weekend relaxing in his yard. I will refer to this man as Ron, although this is not his real name. Ron lived in one of the suburbs of San Diego, in a home located in the country. Please remember that a good deal of San Diego County, during the sixties, was country and not nearly as congested as it is today. Anyway, the nearest neighbor happened to live approximately a quarter mile from Ron and this neighbor had been working on and off for a week trying to remove the stump of a huge oak tree that had died. He had cut the tree down and further cut what had fallen into firewood. He was now taking on the more difficult job of cutting thru the aged root system so he could remove and burn the stump.

Ron, who had recently moved into his home, sat in the front yard watching with interest when he heard the sound of a small explosion. He looked more closely and after the dust had settled Ron could see his neighbor slide into a hole, he had dug around the base of the tree stump, then scramble out and run a short distance and crouch down behind his pick-up truck. Several minutes passed and another small explosion occurred and this peeked even further Ron's interest. After two more explosions Ron realized he just had to get involved. If nothing else, he should at least go over, introduce himself, and offer his expertise.

Ron arrived shortly after another small explosion and made his introduction. He found that the neighbor had been trying to blast through the root system by using quarter sticks of dynamite. This was to be a laborious process and Ron could see very little, if any, headway being made toward removing the stump when he entered the hole to take a peek. The two men set talking and getting to know one another when Ron dropped the bomb, excuse the pun, on his neighbor. He explained that he was a member of the Underwater Demolition Teams and an expert in the fine art of explosives. Ron went on to tell his new friend and neighbor that what he had been doing was all wrong and that he would therefore be only too happy to offer his services; that is, if his neighbor so desired. Ron's neighbor was only too willing to accept the help of one trained in explosives and asked what needed to be done. Mind you, Ron's neighbor had removed tree stumps before, using explosives, but it had always taken a good deal of time because he was very cautious and only used explosives in small amounts. He was however, open for suggestions.

With that Ron asked how much dynamite remained and was pleased to hear that there was nearly half a box, or roughly thirty sticks at his disposal. Ron explained that he would rig the explosives, by running a trunk line, so all of the dynamite could be detonated at one time. The neighbor was somewhat reticent but Ron assured him that he knew what he was doing and that he should just relax and enjoy the moment. Just to be safe, and to further put his neighbors mind at ease, Ron said he would return to his home and bring back a heavy-duty tarp that could be put over the stump. This would contain any dirt and gravel that might otherwise be blown into the air. It took a little more persuading before the neighbor finally agreed and then, only after Ron had recalled some of the major operations, involving explosives that he had been assigned to while in the Teams. With the neighbor now feeling a little less apprehensive Ron returned home to pick up the tarp.

It wasn't long before Ron returned and started setting the explosives that would take care of this simple matter. The neighbor stood by anxiously watching as Ron attached all of the dynamite to the trunk line then exited the hole. Both men then stretched the tarp over the tree stump and staked it to the ground. Ron was now ready to light the fuse and as the neighbor retreated to a shed, a short distance from where his pick-up truck was parked, made a final comment; "I sure hope you know what you're doing." With that, Ron lit the fuse and ran to where his neighbor waited.

Both men now crouched beside the shed anxiously waiting for the explosion that would bring to an end this matter of "the old oak tree." However, what was about to happen was totally unexpected. The huge explosion that followed startled Ron and nearly gave his neighbor a heart attack. There had been more than enough explosives to separate the trunk from its roots. In fact, when they first looked at the sight where the tree trunk had been just seconds before, there was nothing but a gaping hole. They looked at each other; then their attention was quickly diverted skyward. To their surprise the huge tree trunk, which took on the appearance of an incoming missile, was now descending rapidly from the sky, still wrapped securely in Ron's heavy-duty tarp. Next came a loud crushing sound as the tree trunk landed square on top of the pick-up truck, shattering the windows and smashing the truck as flat as a tortilla. Everything was deadly silent for the next several seconds as both men crouched there staring in disbelief at the aftermath of what had just happened. Then, Ron stood up, brushed himself off and said something to the effect; "you don't have to thank me, you can keep the tarp, and isn't that my wife I hear calling me home for diner." With that Ron could be seen running down the road toward his house and the story ended. I never was to hear what happened to the short-lived friendship, formed that day, between Ron and his neighbor. It was however an interesting story and one I enjoyed, have laughed about on numerous occasions, and have never forgotten.

Though this is not an example of the type of story that contains a life-enriching lesson, there would be other stories that would serve us well. From these other stories we would learn the intended lesson, a lesson that could possible save our lives as well as the lives of fellow Teammates. The one thing I do know; not all knowledge can be gained through first hand experience, much has to be acquired by means of a story.

19. TESTING NEW EQUIPMENT

As a member of Underwater Demolition Team Twelve (UDT-12), one of the hardest but most rewarding Team assignments was that of testing new, recently developed "Naval Special Warfare" equipment. During the early to mid-1960's, there would be many challenges associated with testing new, never before seen diving equipment, swimmer recovery platforms, jet boats, swimmer propulsion units, and swimmer delivery systems that were being introduced to the Teams for the first time. Some of this equipment would pass with flying colors and is still being used in the Teams today. Some would be only partially successful and therefore rejected or returned to the manufacturer for modification. Other equipment would fail miserably but often times, not before taking the lives of some very good men. This is the story of one piece of new diving equipment and of the men who volunteered to test that equipment to the limits of its capability and sometimes their own.

During BUDS we had been qualified in the use of both open and closed circuit diving equipment. Most familiar would be the Aqua-Lung, used widely by the military and civilians alike. Not so familiar, to civilian divers, was the closed circuit equipment first introduced during World War II. Unlike the aqua-lung, which provides a constant supply of compressed air, a closed-circuit unit supplies oxygen to the diver, not air. In a closed-circuit system, dispelled air from the diver's lungs is filtered through a canister, filled with an alkaline substance such as baralime that removes carbon dioxide. The purified oxygen then passes into a breathing bag and is supplied once again, as needed, to the diver. The advantage gained by using the closed-circuit system is that there are no tell tale bubbles, to give the diver's position away, and the length of a dive can be extended to 90-minutes, even up to two hours. The disadvantage of using a closed-circuit system; the depth a diver may safely descend is limited to twenty-five feet. Beyond twenty-five feet, the diver will suffer from oxygen poisoning. During training, we were introduced to the Pirelli, the first closed-circuit system developed for the military. However, we trained and qualified using the Drager and Emerson Closed-Circuit Systems.

    In July 1962, members of Class-28 made their transition from BUDS Training to the Teams. At that time, there was a new semi-closed system, the Mark-V, going through rigid testing. While some of the components were similar to those used in closed-circuit equipment, this new system was designed to use mixed gases, mixtures of nitrogen and oxygen, and would allow divers to descend to depths as great as 300 feet. As with the closed-circuit system, a canister filled with baralime would remove carbon dioxide, dispelled when the diver exhales, and allow the then usable mixed gases to return to the breathing bag to be breathed by the diver. One major difference between this system and the closed-circuit system was a pressure release valve, often referred to as a "pop-off valve" by men in the Teams. Later in the story you will find out what caused this name change. The pressure release valve was built into the breathing bag of the Mark-V. The valve is designed to let excess gases escape into the water, as the breathing-bag becomes over inflated. This valve works only one-way, allowing gases to escape while preventing water from entering the bag. By automatically venting excess gasses, the diver can more easily maintain neutral buoyancy without making manual adjustments during a dive. Excess gases in the breathing bag, if not vented properly, could cause the diver to rapidly ascend to the surface and he could then suffer the bends.

    We soon found that there was a major problem, intrinsic to the Mark-V. It was this pressure release valve, a relatively simple piece of equipment, or so you would think. It seems that, on occasion, this valve had a tendency to malfunction, thus preventing excess gases from being dispelled from the breathing bag. When this happened, the breathing bag would over inflate causing the diver to ascend, slowly at first but eventually very rapidly. The mixed gasses would then be forced into the diver's lungs and he would have no way to expel those gases unless he was to remove the mouthpiece. Not removing the mouthpiece, and ascending rapidly without exhaling, could cause the air within the divers lungs to expand beyond his lungs capacity. If this were to happen, the excess mixed gases would be forced through the walls of the lungs and into the blood stream; then into other body cavities causing the diver to suffer from the bends.

On the other hand, if the diver were to remove the mouthpiece, this could then allow water to enter into the breathing system. If the water were to reach the canister, and mix with the baralime, a toxic acid would be activated. If this acid is then forced into the divers mouth, by the pressure built up in the breathing bag, the diver could be severely burned and even die if this substance is swallowed. To prevent water from entering through the mouthpiece, into the breathing bag, a small shut-off device was built into the mouthpiece. When open, the diver can breath normally. When closed, the mixed gas supply stops at the mouthpiece but, because it is closed, water is prevented from entering the mouthpiece and draining down into the breathing bag.

While the proper functioning of these two devices suggests the system is both efficient and fail-safe, there was a hidden problem. As previously mentioned, occasionally the pressure release valve would malfunction. If the diver closed the shut-off device and removed the mouthpiece, the breathing bag would continue to expand until something finally gave. What usually gave first was the pressure release valve that was sewn and glued into the breathing bag. At some point this valve, being the weakest link in the chain, so to speak, would usually be torn loose from the breathing bag. Then, the breathing bag would rapidly fill with water and this added weight would take the diver to the bottom. Because of these inherent problems with the pressure release valve, men in the Teams dubbed it the "pop-off valve" and referred to it as such in all conversations.

We were to encounter this problem during one of our first training dives, using this new semi-closed equipment. We were in the San Diego Bay when one of the new Team-12 divers experienced a problem. The pop-off valve malfunctioned, as it had in the past. When the breathing-bag could no longer expel the gases that were rapidly building up, the diver lost neutral buoyancy. As he ascended ever more rapidly, the breathing-bag reacted like a balloon that is being over filled, it popped. When the breathing-bag reached its maximum capacity the pop-off valve tore free from the system, the air bag filled with water, and the added weight forced the diver to descend once again. By the time he settled on the bottom of the bay, he was unconscious, suffering from the bends, and drowning. When something like this happens, it happens so quickly, a diver has little, if any, time to react. We had been trained to deal with similar problems, how to react without thinking when placed in the most adverse situation, but it hadn't worked this day and sadly, a young classmate died.

Shortly after this incident, several similar problems, all related to the pop-off valve, were encountered and no one could determine why or what caused them. Why would one piece of equipment fail and another work perfectly? Why would one piece of equipment work perfectly on one dive then fail on the next? Adjustments were made and modifications implemented but nothing would correct the problems related to the pop-off valve. We were even encountering problems when testing the equipment in the Amphibious Base Swimming Pool. The one thing we all agreed on; no one wanted to take this equipment on a deep dive. It was tough enough dealing with a system malfunction in the swimming pool, let alone on a deep dive in the unforgiving ocean.

The problems persisted but we continued to dive the Mark-V. Then one night the evil beast struck again. It was 2200 hours, or ten at night, and teammates were swimming simulated sneak attacks on a Navy ship. The ship lay at anchor in the ocean; roughly two miles from the entrance to the San Diego Bay and Harbor. Our UDT pick-up boat would drop off swimmer pairs roughly one-half mile from the ship. The swimmers would then submerge and using their attack boards, swim a compass course to the target ship.

An "attack board" is a piece of wood roughly one and one-half feet long, by one foot wide, by one inch thick. It is painted black with a white stripe down its center. It also has two cutouts, one on each side, to serve as handles. Mounted on the attack board are a magnetic compass, wristwatch, and depth gage. Only one of the two divers is assigned an attack board. The other diver swims slightly above and off of the left shoulder of the diver with the attack board. A piece of nylon line, about three to four feet long, is then tied to one wrist of each diver. This allows the divers to maintain contact in case one diver should lose sight of the other because of poor visibility, or in this case darkness.

The swim teams were deployed at different intervals, and locations, and the night problem was underway. Everything seemed to be going well when, roughly twenty minutes into the operation, the men aboard the pick-up boat could hear cries for help coming from one of the swim pairs. The night was overcast and there was no moon to provide the light needed to locate the surfaced diver or divers. It was also difficult to pin point the direction the shouts were coming from. For five then ten minutes, the men in the pick-up boat could hear the pleas for help but could not locate the distressed swim pair. Then there was silence, there were no further cries for help, the men were gone.

The operation was aborted and the remaining swim pairs were brought back aboard the pick-up boat. Soon, additional Team boats arrived with more men to join in a search that would continue for the remainder of that night, but to no avail. The search was extended for two more days, using all available resources, but the men were never found. Because we could not find our Teammates, it would never be determined what had caused their deaths. What we did know, both men were using the Mark-V; therefore, it could not be ruled out that one of their units had failed.

In early 1963 the Mark-V was formally rejected and replaced by a newer and better Mark-VI system and testing started anew. Initially, there would be problems but none as severe as those encountered when using the Mark-V. It would take a while before we developed complete trust in this new system, but we did and eventually we were using the Mark-VI to make deep ocean dives. I was not one of the first men in the Teams to descend to 300 feet; in fact, my deepest dive, using the Mark-VI, was 180 feet. In the end, it was the men who maintained this equipment, and mixed the gases for these dives, that truly were the heart and soul of this equipment. If it weren't for them, many more young lives might have been lost.

20. HOOYAH! THE WORD

It is my understanding that the word "HOOYAH" was first introduced to the Teams, actually to a BUDS Training class, during the 1950's. Apparently, one of the trainees took the words "Yah Hoo," and simply reversed them, placing the "Hoo" before the "Yah" and then joined the two words together. By the way, "Yah Hoo" would be familiar to anyone who watched 50's era western movies, especially those that involved cattle drives. In those vintage western movies "Yah Hoo" would be guaranteed to get the cattle moving when shouted by the cowboys. In addition, "Yah Hoo" would be the words most often shouted when cowboys rode into town to party on Saturday night. Makes you feel like partying just thinking about it, doesn't it? For those cowboys, "Yah Hoo" was also used for venting (letting off steam) and making their feelings heard; especially feelings of joy when they were given time off from the hardships associated with working on a cattle ranch.

Big deal, so you put one word in front of the other, join those two words together, and create "HOOYAH;" so what? Well, as simple and unimportant as creating this word may sound, "HOOYAH" would have a definite impact on all of the trainees of that BUDS Training Class, when this word was first used. It would also impact every training class that followed. "HOOYAH" would come to be the word that every man who ever entered BUDS Training and then graduated to the Teams grew to deeply understand. Yes, "HOOYAH" is the one word that defines the men who make up the Teams and will always hold special meaning for every man who ever served in the Teams. We will get more into that in a minute.

I have heard some people say that the word "HOOYAH" was taken from the Army Rangers who use the word "HOOAH" as their war cry and is the one word most significant to them. Not true, "HOOAH" gained eminence during the 1960's when the Army Rangers were reintroduced as a segment of the Army Special Forces. While it is true the Rangers were an active unit of the Army during WWII, after the war they were decommissioned and would not be reactivated until their expertise was once again needed in Vietnam.

During the early 1960's when both UDT and SEAL Team members were going through the Army's Jump School, at Fort Benning Georgia, the Army was introduced to the word "HOOYAH" and one assumption is that the word "HOOAH" came into prominence around this time. Rod Powers, an expert on the subject, suggested that the word might have originated during the Civil War, taken from "HOORAY." He also stated that "HOOAH" might have first been shouted during WWII when General Cota posed a question to Rangers of the 2nd Battalion and one of the Rangers answered "WHO US?" Apparently General Cota thought he heard the men shout "HOOAH." While no one knows exactly how the word "HOOAH" came to be, that is certainly not the case with the UDT/SEAL word "HOOYAH."

If you have ever wondered what the word "HOOYAH" actually means, I would have to say that it is the war cry of the Teams and the one word that can be used as a response in many and varied situations but most significantly it means, "YES." During BUDS Training when a trainee is asked a question, by one of the Instructors, the most common response you will hear is that trainee screaming "HOOYAH." During training, "HOOYAH" becomes so ingrained into the mindset of each trainee that the word never leaves his vernacular and from training it is carried into the Teams. What can I say; "HOOYAH" is the word of frogmen.

During BUDS Training, when you are wet, cold, and suffering, which just happens to be all of the time, you need something that will release pent up frustration, something that will help fight off the cold, some way of telling the Instructors that you are still there and that nothing they can do will make you go away or quit the program. Repeatedly shouting out this one simple word, at the top of your lungs, creates a certain magic that helps take your mind off of the cold and all of your suffering. Also, when you hear your fellow classmates screaming the word "HOOYAH," at the top of their lungs, it causes something to happen inside you. You know that these fellow trainees are experiencing the same cold and suffering that you are and that by shouting "HOOYAH" they feel better, that in turn makes you feel better. While this may sound a little strange to those who have never experienced this phenomena, believe me, this truly helps to fight off the cold and suffering and therefore has helped bring many trainees through difficult times.

I always capitalize "HOOYAH" to underscore the importance of the word; simply saying "hooyah" diminishes the feeling of the word and minimizes its true worth. Most importantly, "HOOYAH" is not a word that can be said without feeling. To be shouted properly, "HOOYAH" has to come from your gut, and must resonate from every fiber of your being; it must be shouted with all the mental, emotional, and physical feeling that you can muster. Yes, I did say physical. When you are wet and half frozen, suffering from sleep deprivation, and standing at attention, the word "HOOYAH" is oftentimes the only motivational force you can call on to get you going again. At times like this you have to make it physical, as well as emotional, and believe me you will put your very soul into the effort of shouting this word. For that very reason the word is always capitalized, to do otherwise would just not be fitting or pay justice to "HOOYAH."

In the Teams, "HOOYAH" takes on a whole new meaning. When deploying on a special operation, conducting Team training exercises, or facing a potentially dangerous situation, you always reach back for something to get you going, get the wheels turning, and "HOOYAH" is always there, the one word you can rely on. It is there to help ease the tension associated with facing eminent danger or a difficult challenge. Of course, during stealth operations it would not be prudent to shout "HOOYAH" but at times such as these you can internalize the word, it still works, or at least it did for me.

While I can recall many stories related to the word "HOOYAH," there is one that has often times crossed my mind and I will share that story with you now. UDT-12 had just received a new high-speed boat built from fiberglass composite material. While this in itself was unique, what differentiated this boat from all others was the fact that it was powered by two turbo jet engines. This boat was larger, faster, and a world apart from anything previously used in the Teams. It could sleep two crewmembers and had a small head (bathroom) in the forward compartment. Built into the aft section of the boat was an enclosed swimmer compartment that could accommodate ten swimmers easily and fifteen to twenty, not so easily, but if required. The boat was built for speed; made from light weight fiberglass, and with the power generated from its two turbo jet engines, she proved capable of doing well in excess of 45 knots under ideal conditions. Anyone who ever road this baby can never forget the deafening noise resonating from the two turbo jet engines when she was under full power. All that she was capable of doing and everything happening under your feet, while underway, was truly mesmerizing. As she accelerated, the aft portion of the boat would settle down in the water causing a rooster tail of water that would shoot fifteen feet in the air on ether side of the boat. Yes, this boat was an amazing piece of work and a real attention getter. Each and every time we left the Amphibious Base dock, heads would turn in the direction of this jet-powered demon.

She was literally capable of making the casual observer think that a jet airplane was landing in the bay. It was the ultimate thrill ride, enjoyed by each and every man who ever road her.

Exiting the boat from the aft swimmer compartment, when the boat was underway at full throttle, was an experience unto itself. As the boat picked up speed and neared the designated point of debarkation, swimmers would line up, each with one hand on the shoulder of the swimmer in front. Then, over the roar of the jet engines, you would hear each man shouting in unison, "HOOYAH" over and over again until it built into a grand crescendo. With every shout, the volume grew louder and louder until the chorus of men shouting "HOOYAH" grew even louder than the roar of the engines. Then, as the men exited the boat, each would put one hand behind his head, pushing forward to hold his chin to his chest. This was done to prevent whiplash caused by the impact of his body hitting the water. And, because of the speed of this boat, as close as you would be to the swimmer in front of you when leaving the boat, there would be a distance of twenty to twenty-five feet between swimmers when you finally recovered in the water. It was a new and exciting way to deploy swimmers; it was the way of the future, and the word "HOOYAH" was there.

The question now was; how would a swimmer handle the impact when exiting this craft in full swim gear, with a twin ninety aqua-lung strapped to his back? To answer this question, volunteers would be needed. The request was made, and as was always the case, the young men who had just completed training and entered the Teams raised their hands. Tom Copeland, another member of Class-28, and I would take on this assignment and after the selection had been made there was little argument from those who were not chosen. I think most of the others felt that if someone was to have his head removed, by a twin ninety aqua-lung, better it be one of us than one of them.

Before we get into this story I should introduce you to Tom Copeland. Tom was a hard charger during training and a true operator both during training and in the Teams. He was a man who always gave one hundred percent and one who could always be counted on. He was from Alabama, had that southern drawl, and a great sense of humor. Nothing seemed to bother Tom but when things got tough Tom was one of the men you wanted there beside you. While normally easy going, there would be hell to pay if you wound up on Tom's wrong side. He was as tough as anyone in the Teams and proved this on numerous occasions when someone unknowingly chose him out for a fistfight.

As we climbed into the swimmer compartment and dawned our swim gear it was decided that the first pass would be made at quarter speed. We would progressively work our way to full speed, if it was determined that the initial jumps had been accomplished successfully and without serious injury. Now geared up and ready to go, Tom and I stood in the swimmer compartment and like so many times before started to repeatedly shout "HOOYAH" as we prepared ourselves mentally to exit the boat. On the first and second jump, the aqua-lung banged sharply on the back of the hand that was behind our head to prevent whiplash. Luckily, this contact only caused bruises and minor cuts. When it came time to make the final jump at full speed, I had some serious reservations. Tom on the other hand appeared to be taking everything in his usual easy stride. Then, when the boat reached full speed we both looked at each other as if to say, "what have we gotten ourselves into?" As time to make the fateful jump drew nearer we called upon the one word we knew we could count on and started to build into a repeated and ever increasing roar of "HOOYAH" until it grew so loud that

I think people two miles away could have heard us. With the order to go, and as we started to exit the boat, I could only wonder if I would leave a part or all of my head in the San Diego Bay. Then splash, and to my total surprise this jump was much easier than the previous jumps made at slower speeds. Upon landing, the aqua-lung's harness pulled down on my shoulders and the twin nineties took up most of the impact of hitting the water. For some reason, the higher speed jumps were much easier than those at lower speeds. Tom and I had made it and as we lay there in the water waiting for the boat to circle back to pick us up, we started shouting over and over again the one word that had carried us through this operation, as it had so many others; "HOOYAH."

Yes, "HOOYAH" is the one word that was always there to help me through difficult times. It is a word that will always be a part of me and I am sure there are many others that feel the same as I do. Since the 1950's it has been the one word most often shouted by BUDS trainees and men in the Teams. It will forever be the one word most often associated with frogmen - past, present, and future. "HOOYAH"

Swimmers exiting Swimmer Compartment of one of the Team Boats powered by twin turbo-jet engines.

21. GARY LANPHIER AND THE DEVIL CAR

During the early 1960's, not many of the young men who had just completed BUDS, and entered the Teams, owned his own car. However, for those lucky enough to own a car, the demands of others would be many. Gary Lanphier, a teammate and fellow Class-28 graduate, happened to be one of the lucky few to have his own wheels; he was the proud owner of an old Plymouth. Though it wasn't much to look at, it served him well and proved to be a great means of transportation for many who would have otherwise had to walk, hitchhike, or ride the bus.

Gary was well liked by most of the men who served with him in the Teams. Basically, he was outgoing, animated, and a fun person to be around. Gary was also the person we all liked to pull pranks on and was therefore the brunt of many jokes. However, if you were going to pull a prank on Gary you had better be prepared for the retaliation that would surely follow. With regard to retaliation, Gary always gave at least as much as he received but most often, much more.

During BUDS Training, we would all look at certain individual trainees and try to determine the odds of that person completing the program. There were many who felt Gary had little chance of surviving training but, time and again, he would prove them wrong. Of all Class-28 trainees, Gary possessed the biggest heart, strongest will to survive, and greatest amount of resilience. Gary had what it would take to complete BUDS; he was a warrior.

Gary could easily be compared to one of those little yellow rubber ducks that children take into the bathtub; you could hold him under water for as long as you wanted but as soon as you let him go he would shoot right back to the surface. He was a person that refused to be kept down and he would never go softly or quietly into the night.

Prior to entering BUDS, Gary was a Navy Parachute Rigger and his talents were put to good use at a time when all of the men in the Teams were attaining jump qualification status. He would not only repack our parachutes after a jump, Gary was also responsible for repairing torn or damaged chutes, drying them after water jumps, and a wide assortment of other duties related to his rate.

One day Gary was asked what he would take in trade, for an old unusable parachute that one of the men wanted to convert to a car cover. The Teammate making the request was in charge of an area that served as the Teams garage and repair facility as well as paint shop. Gary in turn said that his car could use a new paint job and if that was acceptable, the deal was on. There was considerable arguing back and forth before a deal was struck and only then because Gary agreed to supply the paint. Shortly thereafter, on a Saturday, Gary turned over the parachute, his car, and enough red paint to do the job twice. Words to the effect, "You could have just as easily given me the parachute" were the final words Gary would hear as he departed for a weekend away from the Team compound and Coronado. Gary then spent the weekend in anxious anticipation of Monday and returning to see his newly painted car. For Gary, this was truly a major happening.

Monday arrived and as everyone gathered for muster, there was a buzz throughout the compound about Gary's car. Men were going to and from the paint shop and all were laughing and talking about what they had just seen. Everyone returned laughing but Gary, he looked like he had just lost his best friend. It wasn't until I went to the paint shop that I realized what had created such a stir and why Gary looked so beleaguered. His car had been painted red all right, and not just the body of the car, the whole car. The chrome, tires, wheels and hubcaps, the bumpers, inside the engine compartment and trunk, even the windows, all painted a fire engine red. It looked like a car driven straight out of the depths of hell. Even today, I can still picture the "devil car"; it was a sight I shall never forget. It was funny to everyone but Gary, and there was nothing he could do about it, the paint had dried hard over the weekend, it was a "done deal".

That afternoon, Gary made up his mind that he would purchase another car and asked if I would go with him to Chula Vista, a suburb of San Diego. I didn't blame him for asking me to come along, I wouldn't have wanted anyone to see me, all alone driving the "devil car" for even a few short blocks, let alone all the way to Chula Vista. In this case, misery truly loved company.

Gary used a razor blade to scrape the paint, as best he could, off of the front windshield on the driver's side. Then, when he tried to start the car the electrical system caught on fire and we were only able to extinguish the fire after a good part of the system was destroyed. Gary's problems had gone from bad to worse but he wasn't nearly ready to surrender. As far as Gary was concerned, he wouldn't let anything this trivial get him down. As we were pondering what to do next, Al Fletcher, another teammate joined in. Then, together we were able to salvage enough of the electrical harness to wire the ignition and starter to the battery and start the car. With that, we rolled down all of the windows and the three of us were under way to Chula Vista. During the drive we encountered many people who took second and even third looks at the "devil car" as we drove past. There were even several cars that nearly ran off the road. Gary was putting on quite a show and everywhere you looked spectators were laughing, but none would laugh as heartily as "Honest John", the car dealer, when we drove into his dealership.

Gary had selected this particular used car lot because the sign out front stated something to the effect, they would not be "under sold" and they were also willing to take any car, "any car", in trade. When "Honest John" saw us coming, I thought he was going to rupture something he was laughing so hard. It was probably five minutes before "Honest John" had calmed down enough so Gary could talk sensibly with him and even then, "Honest John" couldn't get enough of the story; he wanted to know the entire story surrounding the "devil car" and why every square inch of it had been painted red. Eventually he was calm enough to do business and soon after Gary became the proud owner of an Oldsmobile 98 and once again we were on our way. As we drove away from "Honest John's", I looked out of the rear window only to see "Honest John" still standing there, staring at the "devil car" and laughing. I was sure the car would provide many stories for him to tell future customers and friends alike.

It was now early evening so Gary decided we should buy a gallon of wine and catch a drive-in movie to celebrate the purchase of his Olds 98. Gary was just happy that he no longer had to worry about the Plymouth that had, even prior to the paint job, given him problems due to faulty headlight wiring. The car had never been safe to drive at night for fear the lights would go out. This "lights out situation" would happen at the least opportune time, leaving Gary stuck out in the middle of nowhere, and this would happen more often than not. On several occasions Gary had commented that the car had a mind of its own, and he was sure it hated him. But, all of that was behind him; he no longer had to worry, things were starting to look up. What could possibly go wrong now?

We arrived at the drive-in shortly after the previews had started; so, after a quick trip to the snack bar, we settled in to watch the movie. I have never been much of a drinker so passed the gallon of wine to Gary and Al who were sitting in front. It didn't take long before Gary decided that he had satisfied his thirst and gave the bottle to Al to continue on alone. An hour passed and to no ones surprise Al was feeling no pain. We were laughing and joking about what had happened during the day when, out of the clear blue, Al said he was feeling funny and that he thought he was going to be sick. When Gary told him to open the door and get out before something happened, Al took offense to what had just been said and told Gary that he had no right telling him what to do. With that, Al turned his head to the right; then, it looked like someone turned a fire hose on the passenger window, which just happened to be rolled-up at the time. Oh what a mess it made, all that purple wine and hot dog sliding down Gary's window into the door panel and I can't begin to describe the stench.

    At first Gary looked shocked and didn't say anything. There was dead silence for about a minute then Gary simply said, "My car, you ruined my new car". When Gary tried to talk to Al and find out why he hadn't opened the door, Al refused to discuss the matter and again shouted back that Gary had no right telling him what to do. I just sat there in the back seat, and though I tried, I couldn't control my laughter. Surprisingly, Gary didn't try to kill Al, which would have been a normal reaction and one I would have expected; he simply started up the car and said we had to find a filling station. Gary could think of nothing more important than trying to wash the second hand wine and hot dog out of the door panel as he raced out of the drive-in theatre. Needless to say, no amount of water could clean up this mess and no matter how many, green and red deodorant trees Gary put in his car, nothing could remove the smell that had been implanted as a permanent reminder of that evening.

    It didn't take long for Gary to realize that the only way to solve this problem would be by purchasing yet another car and that he did. Wisely, Gary handled this trip alone and I am unaware of any additional problems that accompanied his next purchase. While the problems related to Gary's cars had ended, it would by no means preclude the fact that other problems would soon materialize. It seems that wherever Gary went, problems would surely follow.

22. TO SEA OR NOT TO SEE

Having completed BUDS, all of the enlisted graduates were moved from the training barracks, where we had spent the previous five months, back to the barracks where we were housed for a short time prior to training. This was the early sixties and there were no permanent barracks in the UDT/SEAL Team compound, which is located on the Silver Strand, directly across from the Naval Amphibious Base. In the Team compound there was only enough berthing space to accommodate the duty section, which usually included one officer and six to eight enlisted men. These were the good old days and though the Teams didn't have all of the money that is available to them now, things were getting better.

The barracks to which we were assigned was a relatively new two-story brick structure with windows lining one wall. It was comprised of cubicles, each capable of berthing four men. The building was roughly forty feet wide and eighty to one hundred feet long. There were three isles that ran the length of the building, two on each side and one down its center. On the far end was a head comprised of showers, sinks, and toilets. Each man had his own stand-up locker and they were located along the center isle as well as along the walls at either end of the building. As far as I was concerned it was perfect. The only thing that could have made this situation better would have been having our living quarters located in the Team compound. But, to paraphrase an old saying; "you can't miss what you never had."

I can't remember encountering problems with any of the men that lived in the Team barracks. Sure, you would have to deal with those who came back, after a night on the town, and felt it was their duty to wake everyone and let them know about the good time they had missed. However, this was something that you grew used to and besides, when you are young, events like this don't usually prove to be that vexing. Also, more often than not the barracks was relatively empty. In addition to having a place in the barracks, many of the young men also rented or shared apartments on the beach and only used the barracks to change into their Team uniforms that were stored there. Many others would be deployed on operations or detached on an overseas assignment that could last as long as six months. Basically, the barracks was a good place to be and I was happy there. However, for a two-month period I had rented one of the rooms in a home on the beach leased by Frank Watton another member of UDT-12. This lasted only two months because practically every night when I went into my bedroom I found it occupied by one of my teammates and his lady friend. Not wanting to disrupt what they were doing I would go back to my barracks on the Amphibious Base.

All in all I found it interesting living in this dorm or cubicle environment. However, living this close to the other men makes it difficult to hide any idiosyncrasies you might possess. There were a few men that possessed strange quirks and one of the strangest was that of a man who ran in his sleep. Now I know you have heard of people sleep walking but this was not the case with Glen Luther Jones who was into sleep running. Jones stood at least 6'5" tall and was a gifted athlete. He was the best volleyball player in the Teams, a real achievement when you look at the caliber of athletes that comprise the ranks of the UDT/SEAL Teams. Jones had just one problem; on occasion he would get up late at night and while still sound asleep run head long from one end of the barracks to the other. In itself this was disconcerting enough but it didn't stop there. Glen Luther didn't just come to an abrupt halt when he reached the other end of the barracks, ah contraire, Glen Luther would plow head first into the lockers that lined the wall. Then, as he fell back onto the floor, with a loud thud, the now teetering lockers would fall right on top of poor old Jones. Occasionally, and if he were lucky that night, one of Glen Luther's teammates would reach the lockers before they fell thus preventing Jones further damage. On those instances when Jones wasn't quite that lucky, after the dust had settled, a teammate would drag Jones out from underneath the lockers and deposit him back on his rack or bed. Then, in the morning Glen Luther would have absolutely no recollection of what had happened other than the new black and blue marks, bumps, and abrasions that he couldn't recall being there the night before. Luckily for Jones this didn't happen often but as far as he was concerned it would have been a whole lot better if it didn't happen at all.

Normally, a person is not allowed to join the Navy if that person has a sleepwalking problem. This is understandable because if you were on board a ship you could quite easily walk over the side never to be seen again. However, because Jones never admitted to having this problem he was welcomed with open arms. After earning his berth in the Teams, on all Team related shipboard operations that included Glen Luther, his teammates would take extra precautions to make sure he did nothing that could possibly cause him to fall overboard. They would even go as far as tying a bell to Jones's leg to alert them if he started moving around in the night. Luckily Glen Luther never sustained any major injuries because of this anomaly. He left the service at about the same time I did and with his family moved to Bakersfield, California, an ideal spot to settle down if you happen to be a sleep runner.

Another Team member who always comes to mind when I think about idiosyncrasies is Gary Lanphier. Gary has been the focus of other stories because of the way he dealt with fellow teammates and life in general. Among other eccentricities, Gary possessed the bad habit of coming back from liberty, after a night on the town and having consumed too many bears, then waking everyone in the barracks. Gary was never satisfied with being loud enough to raise the dead, no he had to turn on all the lights and visit every man, badmouthing one after the other until he was satisfied that he had made contact with each and every man in the barracks. After all, Gary didn't want anyone to feel slighted because he had not been included. Then, once he was certain that he hadn't missed anyone he would go to his cubicle and crash. By crash I mean Gary would fall into a deep sleep that was something akin to being dead and once he fell into this all consuming sleep it was then impossible to wake him. Believe me we tried every possible way, on many different occasions, but to no avail. Gary was gone and nothing could disturb him until his internal alarm clock told him it was time to come back to life.

One night after Gary had made his usual rounds and then fallen into this all consuming coma it happened. On this particular evening Ron Tussi and Gary had been in Coronado drinking, fighting, and basically raising hell. They had returned to the base together but after dropping Gary at the barracks, Ron parked his car then stopped at one of the vending machines to purchase an ice cream bar. By the time he entered the barracks Gary had finished making his usual rounds and crashed. Ron went over to wake Gary but no matter how hard he tried Gary refused to budge. Ron then held his ice cream bar over Gary's chest and let the melting ice cream drip down but Gary didn't move. Gary was snoring by this time and was lying on his back with his arms thrust behind his head. Ron then smeared the ice cream on each of Gary's armpits but even then Gary refused to budge. Ron then stood over Gary letting the ice cream drip down on each of Gary's closed eyelids. Still nothing, Gary didn't budge. By now both of Gary's eyelids were covered by pools of ice cream, truly a sight to behold, but still Gary didn't move a muscle. At this point Ron gave up, stuck what remained of the ice cream bar on Gary's chest and went to his cubicle and to sleep. We all had laughed and truly enjoyed what Ron had just done to Gary but knew that the show was now over. With that, we turned off the lights and went to sleep knowing that Gary would bother us no more that night.

Early the next morning I was awakened suddenly by a blood-curdling scream that could have easily awakened the dead. It was Gary and he was running around in a rage repeating over and over that he had gone blind. "I can't see, I'm blind," and all the while Gary was tripping and falling over things, totally out of control. This most assuredly was one of the funniest sights I had ever witnessed. Their stood Gary with what was left of a dried up ice cream bar, stick and all, stuck to his chest and his eyes glued shut by the ice cream that had now hardened. Until Gary could find his way into the head, to wash off this dried up mess, there would be no way for him to open his eyes. One thing, every man that was in the barracks at that moment stood fast, laughing like hell, but unyielding to Gary's pleas for help.

Gary did eventually find his way to the head and was more relieved than angry when he finally washed away the ice cream and was able to open his eyes. He later said that he thought the ice cream was dried blood, from a fight the night before, and that he would surely never see again. After this incident Gary took on a much kinder demeanor but this was short lived. He would remain quiet for the next several days but this was only the respite before the next major storm. Soon Gary was back to his old self and we would once again have to deal with Gary and his next bout of harassment.

23. THAT WAS NO FERRY BOAT RIDE

One of the wildest, most unpredictable, and go-for-broke men that I knew in the Teams was an officer named Mike Paul. When I refer to Teams, I mean Underwater Demolition Teams, more readily known today as Navy SEAL Teams. Mike attended the U.S. Naval Academy, graduated at the top of his class, and was brilliant when it came to mathematically determining how much and where to load explosives to destroy a bridge, concrete bunker, or major obstacle. In dealing with matters that required common sense, that was a whole different matter. In that regard, Mike was somewhat lacking. Please don't take this out of context, when God made Mike, he created a truly talented and gifted individual.

I first met Mike in Yokosuka, Japan, a year before we started training. We were stationed aboard the same ship, a heavy cruiser, but I didn't really get to know Mike until we found out that we were both scheduled to go thru BUDS. It was at this time I found out Mike was different from the other officers I had been acquainted with. He was a party animal and was more comfortable around enlisted men than brother officers. He would go on liberty, get drunk, fight, and generally raise hell with the enlisted men and was well liked and respected by those he chose to deal with. He once took me to an Officer's Club and tried to pass me off as a Naval Officer. I was seventeen and looked no more like an officer than the small children swimming in the pool at the Officer's Club. He cared little for what his peers felt and exhibited the basic mentality that seemed well suited for the Teams.

In anticipation of BUDS training, I worked out and trained the entire year I was in Japan. When Mike heard this, he decided it would be good to join me in my daily workout. This all happened about a month and a half before we were to be shipped out to San Diego and training. I would get up at zero four hundred hours (4a.m.) and wake Mike, or should I say, try to wake Mike. More often than not, he would just be returning to the ship from a night of partying and was seldom in the mood for a long run and Physical Training (P.T.). Those times he did come out with me, I would usually get frustrated with his slow running pace. I would tell him that I would meet him at the base training field, and then I'd take off running by myself. I would then see Mike on the base bus as it traveled the same course that I ran, and he would wave as he passed. Once there, he would do a few exercises, but mostly he would talk and distract me. When it was time to run back to the ship, I would take off, and Mike would wave as the bus passed me on the return trip. I liked Mike, but really didn't think he had a snowball's chance in hell of completing BUDS. Mike and I parted company when I left the ship to take a month leave before reporting to training.

    The first three weeks of BUDS is strictly oriented to physical training, geared toward getting everyone in shape for Hell Week and the real training that would follow. It is extremely hard, and the Instructors are merciless, but that initial three weeks can in no way compare to what would follow. You are not allowed to quit training during those first three weeks, but had it been allowed, probably fifteen to twenty percent of the trainees would have done so.

    I didn't deal with Mike until probably the second week of training when the class was divided into seven-man boat crews. From that point forward, the individual trainee was no more. As a member of a boat crew, you become an appendage of this one body and seven men are taught to think, act, and behave as one. If you fail to do so, you will not make it thru BUDS. At this time I was assigned to Mike's boat crew and from that point forward, I remained with Mike thru the completion of training,

    To my surprise, Mike made it thru Hell Week with flying colors. He was short in stature and of average build, but had a heart as big as anyone I had ever met. I grew to admire and respect Mike as we went further into training and marveled at some of Mike's antics. He was extremely supportive of the men in his boat crew and was always there when we needed him. As a boat crew, we would be required to resolve problems that would leave the other class members scratching their heads. Mike, however, could lead us thru the problem to completion, well ahead of the others; therefore, we would have free time while the others worked. While this was admirable, there were matters relating to common-sense issues that Mike just couldn't deal with. While I could go on and on about them here, I feel it would be better to write about them separately and will do so.

    Mike and I graduated from BUDS, Class-28, in July of 1962 and were both assigned to UDT-12. Mike was given a platoon to command, and I was assigned to that platoon. Mike then went home on leave and returned driving an old Model-T Ford from his high school and pre-service days. Mike was a character to begin with, but in this car, he was a sight to behold, sometimes running totally out of control. He was hell on wheels and always doing something to alienate the Commanding Officer (C.O.) of the Naval Amphibious Base in Coronado. The thing with Mike, once he realized he could get under someone's skin, he wouldn't back off but would rather continue to stick it to that person even harder. So was the case with the Base C.O., Mike was merciless when it came to pushing this man's buttons. Our UDT-12 Commanding Officer was little bothered by what Mike did, but in the Teams, it takes a lot to raise the dander of Team Command.

    It wasn't long before Mike had accumulated numerous traffic citations, both on Base and in town, which provided the Base C.O. with the perfect weapon to strike out at Mike. He ordered Mike to remove his car permanently or be brought up on charges. By remove, I mean get rid of permanently, not just from the base, but also from Coronado, San Diego, and the surrounding vicinity. Mike didn't take this very well, but after racking up a couple more infractions, grudgingly agreed to do as ordered.

Mike felt retaliation was in order and came up with a plan that would deal a blow to the Base C.O., for what he, Mike, felt was unjust and unwarranted punishment. He didn't share his plan with anyone, but members of his platoon would soon be called upon to play a major role in carrying out Mike's plan, or should I say clandestine operation.

The principal component in Mike's plan was a Ferry Boat that transported cars and passengers from San Diego to Coronado and back. This all happened before the bridge connecting Coronado to San Diego was built. It also happened during a period in history when life moved a little more slowly and was lived without so much intensity. The Ferry was slow paced, fun, and provided a leisurely way to travel back and forth between the two cities.

Now, for example, if you were traveling from Coronado to San Diego, and you were driving, you would first line up behind an iron bar, four cars abreast, or behind the car or cars that had already lined up. The iron bar was about three feet high and was placed there to prevent cars from driving into the bay. That bar would only be lowered when all arriving cars and passengers had exited, and it was safe to board the Ferry. When the Ferry arrived on the Coronado side, the cars would exit to the left and right and then drive down a single lane road that then connected to a major street leading into Coronado. The exit road was separated from the cars, waiting to board the Ferry, by a row of shrubs and bushes that stood about eight feet high. After the Ferry had disembarked all of the cars and passengers, the bar would be dropped, and waiting cars and passengers would board the Ferry. This process would continue around the clock, and the number of cars and passengers, making the trip, would vary depending on the time of day.

It is now time to put Mike's clandestine plan into action. Mike first removed the license plates from the old Model-T. He then removed any other form of personal identification. Mike had to be certain there would be a large number of cars and pedestrians, backed-up and waiting for the Ferry, so he now waited for evening rush hour traffic. Then, with the Ferry completely loaded and just leaving the pier, Mike raced down the exit-only road, screaming and honking the horn on his old Model-T in order to attract maximum attention. There was no bar on the exit ramp, because no one had ever made the mistake of boarding the Ferry by driving down the exit-only road. Besides, it was clearly marked "WRONG WAY, DO NOT ENTER, EXITING TRAFFIC ONLY!" So who would ever do something so bizarre?

The Ferry was approximately fifty feet from the pier when Mike reached the end of the road and became airborne. Still honking the horn and screaming for the Captain of the Ferry Boat to wait, he landed in the bay about ten feet from the pier. Then, like a gallant skipper, Mike went down with his ship, or car in this case. Women and children were screaming, and waiting passengers were scrambling out of their cars to take in this horrific sight. By now, the Ferry Boat Captain had been alerted to what had happened and stopped to help recover the poor victim of this terrible incident. No one jumped into the water to rescue the person driving the car and sadly the driver never came to the surface. It was assumed the person had drowned.

Back inside the car, Mike donned a scuba tank, mask, and swim fins he had placed there earlier and waited for the car to sink to the bottom. He then escaped thru an open window and swam underwater, down the beach, where he came ashore. He returned to the Team Compound, showered, and changed into his uniform just in time to receive a call from the Coronado Police Department, asking for assistance in a body recovery. From the men on duty, Mike assembled a recovery team, the necessary diving equipment, and headed out to answer this call for help.

By the time we arrived, a huge crowd had gathered, including members of a local Television Station. Mike assured all those present that he and his men would recover the body, but sadly, the man had been in the water far too long and surely had drowned. Body recovery was a normal assignment for all men in the Teams, so it was handled routinely until we were in the water and realized that the car we were looking at belonged to Mike. At that point Mike signaled for us to surface. On the surface he told us not to say anything and just go along with what ever he said. We agreed and continued the search for the body that wasn't there. We continued the search until our air supply was exhausted. At that point Mike told the police we would have to return to the Team Compound, replenish our air supply, and then return to continue the search.

It was about twenty hundred hours or eight in the evening when we arrived back at our team compound to recharge our tanks. By now the Base Commander had been briefed by the local police and had assured them they would receive all of the support they required. The News Media and Television had now been added to the equation, not only at the dive site, but also at the Naval Amphibious Base. When we arrived, they were interviewing the Base C.O., who relished all of the attention now being lavished upon him. However, he wasn't happy when he learned that Mike Paul was the Duty Officer and man leading the recovery effort. He pulled Mike aside and asked for his assurance that he would do nothing to embarrass him or his Command. Mike looked directly into the eyes of the C.O. but said nothing. He then turned to Jim Foley and me, winked, gave us a big smile, and walked away. The C.O. then went back to more important matters, his interview, and appeared to put Mike out of his mind.

It was approximately twenty-two hundred hours when we arrived back at the dive site. The police were there with a tow truck and asked us to attach a line to the car so it could be pulled from the water. Mike eagerly agreed and, in a very short time, the car was resting on the beach. I knew it was all over now, but Mike calmly ordered us back into the water to continue our body search. The press, and those bystanders who had remained, looked over the car with renewed interest. Then, when the recovery team ran low on air and returned to the beach, we noticed a couple of men from the Teams. They had seen some of what had happened on TV and were there because they had recognized Mike's car. I thought they were going to die laughing when they realized what we were doing. I then thought this would surely give us away, but it didn't, at least not at that moment.

With no license plate, or any other form of identification, the police officer stated that they would have to trace the car through DMV records, using the vehicle identification number as their only source of available data. Anyway, they said they would start working on it immediately. One of the police officers said he thought he recognized the car as one he had seen driving thru Coronado. He then stated that he would go back to the station and research the records. We listened intently as Mike smiled at the officer, and I knew at that moment it was all over.

When the officer returned, he was apparently upset. He then asked Mike to step aside, and the officer went at Mike with a fury of words I couldn't quite make out but knew weren't flattering. Apparently, it hadn't been necessary to trace the car thru the DMV. Because of the various traffic citations Mike had incurred, during his escapades in Coronado, several of the officers on duty had recognized his car. By midnight, everyone was aware that Mike had perpetrated this hoax; the only question now was what to do about it.

At this point, everyone thought that what had happened was just another prank, contrived by members of the Teams. This wasn't an unusual event; it just happened to be one of the better pranks perpetrated by one of the frogmen. The police had started to lighten up and see the humor in what had happened, and the press played the incident up as one the greatest hoaxes of all time. The Commanding Officer of UDT-12 didn't seem too upset; after all, this type of independent thinking wasn't uncommon among highly motivated men, men like those that comprise the ranks of the UDT/SEAL Teams. After all, it's this ability to develop and carry out unorthodox plans during battle that saves lives. It seems everyone was willing to let it slide, everyone that is except the Commanding Officer of the Amphibious Base who had been embarrassed by the incident. He wouldn't be satisfied with anything less than Mike's blood. As far as the Teams were concerned, the C.O. of the Amphibious Base wasn't directly responsible for Mike or any member of the Teams. However, he did have something to say about where we were housed on his base, and he used this as a club to see that Mike was punished for his reckless actions.

To resolve the matter, Mike was sent to Cuba. He would head up a detachment of men, in response to President Kennedy's order to deploy troops and combat the Cuban Missile Crisis. Three months would pass before Mike would once again return to Coronado. During those three months, life in and around Coronado and the Amphibious Base slowed to normal once again. By this time, the issue of Mike's car was history, and the Commanding Officer of the

Amphibious Base was satisfied that Mike had received adequate punishment. I am certain that the C.O. even felt that he had won. But, little did he know what Mike had in store for him once he returned to the Amphibious Base with his new Triumph Motorcycle.

24. 1962 AND THE CUBAN MISSILE CRISIS

July 1962 – J.F.K. was our President, John Glenn was the first American to orbit the earth, and I had just completed Basic Underwater Demolition SEAL Training (BUDS). For most of you, completing BUDS may not rate up there with Kennedy or Glenn, but for me it was the accomplishment of a goal and the fulfillment of a dream. I was in the Teams, a member of Underwater Demolition Team-12 (UDT-12), one of the Navy's Special Operation Units, known today as Navy SEALS.

In the Teams, when you are not on a Special Operation or attending classes, to hone your combat skills, you are required to spend each day working out. Imagine that, being paid to workout, do all the things I loved. Each day, we reported in at zero seven hundred hours or seven a.m., followed by Physical Training (P.T.) and a swim or run. Then we were free to lift weights, play volleyball, handball, run, swim, surf, or any other activity, as long as it addressed physical fitness. In addition, there were classes in Judo, Karate, and other Martial Arts. Life was good, and I was very content. This was the life I had dreamed of; this was where I belonged, where I wanted to be.

My first two months in the Teams went by quickly and before I knew what had happened, it was September, and our peaceful world was caught up in chaos. The winds of war were starting to blow from Cuba and onto the eastern shore of the United States. Those winds would soon turn into a full-fledged hurricane as Russia inserted both long and short-range nuclear missiles into the equation. To all Americans, the hurricane would soon be known as the "Cuban Missile Crisis."

In late September, a detachment of men from UDT-12 received orders to report immediately to a ship in San Diego harbor and then leave for Cuba.

President Kennedy had ordered a blockade to prevent additional Russian ships from entering Cuban waters. I was elated to be a part of that detachment and looked forward to putting into practice all that I had learned in BUDS. As a nineteen year old, I didn't fully grasp the gravity of the situation and honestly, I don't believe there were many Americans who truly understood how close we were to a full-blown nuclear war.

Literally hundreds of U.S. Navy ships, from both the East and West coast, were ordered to set sail for Cuba. Thousands of Marines boarded the transport ships and by the time we got underway, San Diego looked like a ghost town. As we left port, I can remember how eerie it seemed; there were no Navy Ships in a usually crowded San Diego harbor.

Without much fanfare, we passed thru the Panama Cannel and soon were in Cuban waters. It wasn't long before we encountered a Russian freighter, and the Captain of our ship sounded General Quarters. All hands went to their battle stations, and the detachment from UDT-12 was ordered below deck. Now, to put a new edge on the situation, one of the ship's lookouts spotted the periscope of a submarine. We had been informed that there were no American submarines in the area; therefore, it could only be one thing, Russian. I don't have to tell you that being below deck, with a Russian submarine nearby, wasn't the place that any of us wanted to be. It was decided that our best bet would be to gather our swim gear and move to the fantail, or the aft part of the ship. This way we could keep an eye on things and if the Submarine fired a torpedo at us, we could swim the rest of the way to Cuba. In reality, that would have been highly unlikely because up to that point, we had not yet seen land.

Being on the fantail of the ship did, however, provided the best seats in the house for what was about to happen. The submarine did little more than follow us at a distance while our Ship's Captain took charge and ordered the Russian freighter to turn around and set sail for home. That did little to influence the Russian Skipper to leave the area, so our Captain fired a five-inch burst across the bow of the Russian Freighter. Now, that was language the Russian understood, and he immediately made a perfect u-turn and left the area. With that, the submarine departed our company, and the Russian ship disappeared over the horizon.

Day turned into night as we made our way to Guantonimo Bay, which is the American Naval Base in Cuba. We passed what must have been a hundred ships, entered the bay and docked at the only pier. I remember thinking, how fortunate for us, allowed to pull alongside a pier, while all the ships we had passed were required to lay at anchor offshore. I never did find out the reason for this, but I felt it must have been a good omen.

Upon arrival, the first thing we learned was that all military families living on the base had been flown back to the United States, leaving only Navy and Marine Corp personnel behind. Most of the Marines had been dug-in along a fence line that separates the Naval Base from Cuban occupied territory, and most had been at their post for nearly a month, without relief. Command decided that these men were to be relieved by Marines from one of the ships anchored offshore. Command then decided that a good way to take the edge off of this tense situation would be by hosting a smoker, or series of boxing matches. All base personnel, Marine and Navy, would attend, and they would be given all the free beer they could drink. The UDT-12 detachment was invited to attend the gala event and accepted with much enthusiasm.

Now I ask you, what was the genius who came up with this idea thinking? All the free beer you can drink, Navy and Marine Corps personnel together, an already tense situation, and boxing matches. All the ingredients needed to make a bomb and free beer intended to serve as the fuse. Now, for those of you who don't know this, Sailors and Marines mix about as well as a can of gas and fire; when mixed together you can count on an explosion. So, as you might have guessed, the best was yet to come.

We left the ship and walked over a hill and about a mile to the area where a boxing ring and about four hundred chairs had been set up. There was even a table adorned with fishing poles that would be given to each winner of the planned bouts. We were among the first to arrive, and the Base Officers were standing around congratulating themselves on the "great event" they had put together on such short notice. As I look back on that evening, I would have to say that it did turn out to be an event I remember vividly to this day. "Great event," that's questionable.

As everyone started to arrive, you could feel tension mount between Marine and Navy personnel stationed at the base. It had been predetermined that the boxing matches would pit a Marine against a Sailor so, as you can see, the plot was starting to thicken. As the size of the crowd grew, so too did the amount of beer being consumed. As each bout concluded and the next began, the crowd became more and more inebriated. By the time of the final bout, or main event of the evening, there had been several fights involving spectators that turned out to be much more exciting than those in the ring. Then, as they announced the main event, there was only one boxer, the Marine, standing in the ring. It appeared that Sergeant Tolliver had been the Marine Corps light heavyweight champion and when his opponent found out that fact, he decided to withdraw from the bout. At that point, the announcer asked if there was a Sailor in the house willing to take on the Marine champion.

The next thing I knew, Sonny Smith, from UDT-12, was standing in the ring dressed in his jump boots and green khaki pants, having already removed his shirt. Now I said standing, but that is somewhat of an overstatement. Sonny was about three shades in the wind and staggering is closer to what he was doing, not standing. Everyone in the crowd cheered as Sonny slapped his boxing gloves together, and Sergeant Tolliver sparred and danced in his corner. The referee brought both men to the center of the ring, gave them instructions about keeping it a clean fight and sent them back to their respective corners to await the bell. The bell rang, and both men moved toward each other, Tolliver dancing and gliding, hands held high, Sonny just kind of staggering, hands about waist level. Then, as they met at center ring it happened, Sonny brought his right leg back and, with all the power he could muster, kicked Tolliver in the crotch with such force the Sergeant was lifted at least three feet into the air. The look of pain on his face and the crunching sound made as Sonny's boot came in contact with Tolliver's groin brought an OHHH from the crowd and then total silence. Total silence that lasted for all of three seconds, and then the fight to end all fights was underway. Sonny in the ring, standing triumphantly, Tolliver agonizing on the ring canvas, and four hundred Sailors and Marines going at each other with a vengeance. It looked like something straight out of an old western movie. Fists and chairs flying, and officers running for cover. In the confusion, men were running off with the fishing-pole trophies, and I don't mean the men who had won them in the ring. Everywhere you looked, Sailors were fighting Marines, and there were even cases where Sailors were fighting Sailors and Marines fighting Marines. We had been sent to Cuba to prevent World War III, but at that moment, it looked as though WW III was well underway. What would Castro have said, had he known?

    The fighting lasted for what seemed an eternity and when the smoke cleared, there were bodies everywhere. Some of the men were still partying and enjoying the free beer, many more were still trying to figure out what had happened. Jim Foley, another Teammate, and I climbed into the ring, removed Sonny, and started back to the ship. We had enjoyed the evening and the show Sonny had provided but decided that, like all good things, this too must end. Actually, we felt it would be wise to get the hell out of there before the base officers started looking for someone to blame.

As we were walking along the road, which led back to our ship, a large deuce and a-half (military truck) filled with Marines passed us. The men were laughing and singing, and most were intoxicated. As they passed, one of the Marines shouted, "Hey, ain't that the guy who just kicked the shit out of Sergeant Tolliver?" Well, I have to admit, the sound of those few words made the hair on the back of my neck stand on end. Here we were, the three of us, and there they were, twenty-five to thirty Marines. When they told the truck driver to stop, I knew we were in for a fight that would make the fight we had just left seem like a Sunday picnic.

The men started climbing over each other to get to us, and we just stood there waiting for the inevitable. At this point, something very strange happened. The men all went for Sonny, but instead of tearing him apart, they lifted him onto their shoulders, screaming and shouting his praises and treating him like a long lost brother. Jim and I stood there in disbelief as the Marines carried Sonny around and then hoisted him up into the back their truck. They then told us to climb aboard so they could give us a ride back to our ship. When we got underway, they shared their reason for treating us in such a non-confrontational manner; after all, we were then and would remain sworn enemies.

Apparently, Tolliver was their First Sergeant and a person who none of them cared for or respected. He was a sadistic individual who took great pleasure in mentally and physically abusing them and was, therefore, disliked by all of his subordinates. They had hoped against hope that someone, like Sonny, would come along and take care of their nemesis. Tonight, their prayer had been answered. To show their appreciation, they gave Sonny a bottle of rum that everyone shared on the way back to the ship. Now, as I look back on my years in the service, I can't recall many good times spent with Marines. However, during that short ride, I truly felt camaraderie with those men. We all shared one thing in common, the realization that Sonny had done something extraordinary that night.

We stayed at the Naval Base for the better part of a week but were restricted to ship, barred from going ashore. The Base Commander had felt that we were responsible for the fracas at his smoker and didn't want another incident. As far as we were concerned, we had certainly had enough fun that one evening ashore to satisfy us for at least a week. We were, therefore, little bothered by the restriction.

With regard to the Cuban Missile Crisis, it seems the pressure President Kennedy applied thru the blockade worked. It forced the Russians to the table where an agreement was reached and the missiles removed. With that behind us, we then shipped out for the Virgin Islands to conduct mock assault landings, thru a joint force exercise. With so many troops together at one time, from all branches of the military, Command felt it was a good opportunity to conduct training exercises in anticipation of the next war, Vietnam.

Upon conclusion of the joint exercises, we returned to our homeport, Coronado, California, where we arrived just before Christmas. My life in the Teams would be filled with many unforgettable events, but for now a very memorable 1962 had concluded.

25. BODY SEARCH - PANAMA

Dealing with the dead is always a little disconcerting; but for some this undertaking poses a much bigger challenge than it does for others. In the Teams each man was called upon to perform this task and eventually each grew accustomed to diving for and recovering victims of drowning. Although this was never a task that any of us grew fond of, it was just part of the life that we had chosen and therefore when called upon to perform body search and recovery, like it or not, most of us just did it. For some however, body search and recovery was a part of the job they would much rather leave in the hands of others.

Tom McDonald (Mac) was a second-class petty officer and as tough an individual as you would want to meet. He did have one hang up however, diving for and recovering dead bodies. As far as Mac was concerned, he would much rather grapple with a mountain lion than dive for a victim of drowning. Whenever Mac was forced to go on a body search he always tried to persuade the officer in charge of the dive to let him coxswain the boat and assign someone else to recover the victim. It seems that Mac was superstitious about certain things and diving for, or in any other way dealing with, the dead ranked at the top of his list of superstitions.

On our way to Cuba, in support of the Cuban Missile Crises, the ship that was transporting our UDT Detachment was required to navigate the Panama Cannel. This was interesting, exciting, and a real experience for all of us and we remained topside during most of this nine-hour crossing. As we approached the Panama Cannel, from the Pacific Ocean, we were first required to transverse a seven-mile stretch to reach the first of two locks that would raise our ship roughly fifty feet. Once through the first two locks we then sailed through a long cannel that had been cut through the Continental Divide. The cannel eventually opened up onto Gatun Lake, a twenty-three mile long lake formed by the Gatun Dam. The Gatun Locks, a series of three locks that would drop our ship some eighty-five feet to the Atlantic Ocean, awaited us on the far side of the lake. However, before we made our way through the Gatun Locks, we would spend the night anchored in the lake near Panama City.

    We were all excited that we would spend this one night here and hoped that we would be allowed to visit Panama City and experience some of what the city had to offer. We had all heard many stories about Panama's night life and couldn't wait to see if those stories were true of just the fabrications spun by other sailors prone to exaggerating things they had seen and done. To our dismay we were not allowed to spend any liberty time in Panama because we were to get underway very early the next morning and it was feared that we might not return on time. That night, from the deck of the ship we could see the lights of the city beckoning us to come ashore and also hear the merriment from those enjoying all that Panama had to offer. Oh well, this would have to wait for another day, possibly upon our return trip and if not then; Panama would still be there when we returned for jungle warfare training.

    Most of us would find it difficult to sleep that night, not because the city beckoned us to come taste her wares, but because of the heat. Having left a much cooler climate in San Diego, only days earlier, it would take a while before we could acclimate our bodies to this wearing heat and high humidity, two extreme factors you just don't experience in San Diego. Then, at about 0300 hours or three in the morning, Chief Corey came into our compartment, turned on the lights, and ordered all hands on deck. A young Marine, who had been drinking in Panama City, upon returning to his ship fell off of a pier and drowned. Apparently he had been sitting on the pier when he fell forward then down approximately thirty feet, hitting his head on one of the logs used as a bumper to prevent a ship from bouncing against the pier. He had gone under immediately and did not resurface so it would be our job to initiate a standard body search and recovery.

    Seven swim pairs were selected and we quickly gathered all of the gear we would need for this dive. By the time we reached the fantail, or aft portion of the ship, one of our boats, a "Landing Craft Personnel Recovery" (LCPR) was being lowered over the side and into the water. As we made our way to the starboard side of the ship to board our LCPR, we could hear an argument between Mac and a first class petty officer about who would be the boat coxswain. Actually it was more pleading from Mac than arguing. Because Mac was a second-class petty officer, he was out ranked by the first-class who insisted that he would coxswain the boat that night. This then would mean that Mac would have to join the dive. We all got a good laugh out of what was happening; we knew how Mac felt about diving for a body, especially if diving for the victim had to be done at night and in water that did not provide good visibility. Mac lost this battle and no matter how hard he pleaded he was unable to convince the first-class that he should be the boat coxswain. Mac wasn't going to give up that easily and spent the next ten minutes, while we made our way to the pier, trying to convince Chief Corey that he should be allowed to remain in the boat and that he wasn't really needed in the water. Chief Corey was a fair man but he wouldn't give in to Mac's pleading. Mac lost on all counts when the Chief assigned him to be in the first swim pair to enter the water and start the search. We all got a real laugh out of this, everyone but Mac that is.

    The rest of the men were then paired up, given their assignments and started entering the water at various locations near the pier. Each man would be wearing an aqua-lung comprised of twin tanks, commonly referred to as a twin-nineties, plus diving weights, a k-bar knife, fins, face mask and wet suit top. Out of water, the twin-nineties were awkward and heavy, weighing in at between eighty and ninety pounds. However, once in the water the tanks became buoyant and you would hardly notice that you had them strapped to your back. Once geared up and ready, each swim pair was given a long metal steak with a line or rope attached. Each pair would now enter the water and drop straight down to the bottom. Once on the bottom, the steak would be pushed into the mud. Each steak had a twenty-foot length of line or rope attached and while remaining, as close to the bottom as possible each pair would swim in an ever-widening circle until they reached the end of their line. Because of the darkness it would be important to remain on the bottom and feel your way along; this would provide your only hope of coming in contact with the body should it be in your assigned area.

Soon, seven pairs of swimmers were underwater, in their assigned areas and combing the bottom for the young Marine. If the body was found and brought to the surface, the remaining swim pairs would be informed by one of the boat crew who would pound on the side of the LCPR. Three times then a short break followed by pounding three more times until all swim pairs had returned to the surface. Now if you think about it, Mac's chances were one in seven that his pair would find the body, so you might say he shouldn't have worried. But worry or not, as luck would have it, or should I say, as fate would have it, Mac and his partner were the ones to find the young Marine. What was now about to happen would forever be remembered by those men assigned to this body search and recovery and it is talked about to this day.

I had been in the water with my swim buddy, Jim Foley, for roughly twenty minutes when we heard the signal to surface. When we reached the LCPR half of the swim pairs were in the boat, as was the young marine who was now covered by a blanket. Mac was as far aft in the LCPR as he could get without falling overboard. Also, he was there because this was as far away from the body as was possible. Tied alongside the LCPR was an Inflatable Boat Small (IBS), or rubber raiding craft, used in the Teams to insert five to seven operatives, onto a beach, during a sneak and peak operation. The purpose of the IBS on this operation was to make it easier for the swimmers to enter and exit the water, at the beginning and completion of the dive, due to the weight of the diving tanks. Now, though I wasn't a first hand witness it didn't take long before everyone was aware of what happened when Mac and his swim buddy found the body.

It seems that Mac and his partner had completed three revolutions when Mac ran head first into the body. Though you couldn't see anything in the darkness his partner swore that when he looked at Mac he could see two huge eyes that almost covered the inside of his face mask. The next thing his partner saw was a pair of fins streaking to the surface followed by a steady stream of bubbles. On the surface Chief Corey and the first-class boat coxswain were startled to see a swimmer come shooting out of the water. Even with the weight of the twin-nineties on his back Mac came out of the water to just above his knees and directly into the IBS without so much as touching its side. This would be an impossible feat to duplicate and to this day no one knows how he was able to accomplish it. Now if you are wondering how Mac was able to surface from roughly fifty feet of water, at this breakneck speed, without getting the bends, that is simple to answer. From the second he came in contact with the body until he was in the IBS, he was screaming at the top of his lungs. Mac wasn't inhaling; he was in fact exhaling much faster than the air in his lungs could expand. And from what the others said, he was still screaming after climbing over the gunnels and into the LCPR. In fact, he didn't stop screaming until he reached the back of the boat where he was sitting when Jim and I climbed aboard.

    The entertainment provided by Mac and the body search was now history so after returning the young Marine to his ship we returned to ours. As for Mac, he wouldn't sleep that night or for several nights to follow. This had really gotten to him but it too would pass. The next morning we made our way through the three Gatun Locks and were soon steaming in the Atlantic Ocean, making our way toward Cuban waters. Our ship would now become a part of a blockade that would prevent Russian ships from entering Cuban ports with their cargo of nuclear missiles. While our passage through the Panama Cannel had been exciting and fun it could in no way compare to what awaited this detachment of frogmen who were to now become a part of "The Cuban Missile Crises."

26. ICE CREAM AND STRAWBERIES

As a little boy I had lost my taste for ice cream and as strange as that may sound it is nonetheless true. My father drove a milk route for IXL, a local producer of dairy products in Colorado Springs. This provided the family with all of the dairy products we needed, including ice cream. If the ice cream sat in the delivery truck for too long and started to melt, it would then be considered unfit for delivery or sale and the employees would be allowed to take it home to their families. At first this was like heaven for my sister and me but in time I lost my taste for ice cream, having over indulged to the point of being sick on several occasions. In time I gave up eating ice cream altogether and strange though it may be, I reached a point where I could barley stand the thought of taking another bite of this creamy substance. As I grew older I would overcome my aversion to ice cream but I would never again acquire a passion or craving for this frozen delicacy.

The only other eatable that I can recall having an aversion to was strawberries and again that came through overindulgence. My family had visited friends who had a strawberry patch and of course offered us all the strawberries we could eat and/or take home with us; we just had to pick them. My parents picked a couple of small boxes then went back to visit with their friends. Not me, I had no interest in listening to adult dribble, not when I could be outside eating strawberries. I declined the offer to come inside and just continued to pick, wash, and eat strawberries until I thought I would explode. I remember thinking that if I were in heaven, it couldn't be any better than this. When I could eat no more I noticed a redness starting to cover my arms and legs and knew that I had done something terrible and this was God's way of punishing me. A severe stomachache would accompany the rash and both were intended to prevent me from ever becoming a strawberry glutton. The rash was a real nuisance but within a day it was gone, so to the stomachache. Gone too was my desire for strawberries and to this day it has not returned.

    Years would pass and I would find myself in the Teams, headed for Cuba in response to the Cuban Missile Crises. A detachment of men from UDT-12 had received orders to board a small high-speed destroyer, and as expeditiously as possible get underway and into Cuban waters. We were to support the blockade of Cuba, imposed by President Kennedy. The blockade had been ordered to prevent Russia from shipping additional missiles to Cuba, missiles that could then be used to target the United States. An American U-2 aircraft had taken pictures, while flying over Cuba, that did show there were already short-range missiles in place that could easily reach the East Coast of the United States. Later reconnaissance missions would reveal that long-range missiles were also being installed. Herein lay the real problem. These long-range missiles possessed the capability of reaching every major city in the United States including cities on the West Coast. To combat this crisis President Kennedy was busy trying to negotiate the removal of these missiles and it was the job of the blockade to prevent any additional missiles from reaching Cuban Ports.

    Our ship had departed San Diego Harbor in such a hurry that we hadn't time to properly load all of the necessary provisions required for a prolonged operation. Therefore, when we arrived in Cuban waters and took up our appointed blockade station, the Captain of our ship sent out an urgent call for food supplies. In response to this request, a Navy supply ship was dispatched, came alongside, and started the procedure of high lining or transferring the much-needed food supplies from the supply ship to our ship.

Food is highly important to all those who serve in the military but none more so than the men in the Teams. Therefore, I wasn't surprised when Chief Corey ordered all hands on deck to assist in loading the transferred food from the deck of the ship to the refrigeration compartment and food locker. During this transfer process someone came up with a brilliant idea that would surely benefit the UDT detachment. This idea was perpetrated on the conclusion that there remained an underlying possibility that the ship could run out of food once more and if that were to happen we would all go hungry. To prevent this potential disaster it was decided that we would not take all of the food to the ship's refrigerator and/or food locker. We would instead transfer some of the food to our UDT berthing compartment. There it would be safely stored for future consumption, by the UDT detachment, in case we were to run up against another food shortage. Sounded like a good plan to me.

As the line of men, carrying the goods to the refrigerator and food locker, snaked its way down the passageway, twenty cases would be moved directly to the ship's store-rooms while one case would find its way to the UDT compartment. Then, thirty to forty cases to the ship's pantry and one case to the UDT compartment and so on and so on. When this task was finally concluded, we looked on proudly at the small stash of goods we had moved to our compartment. Then, when it was all surveyed and safely stowed we set back triumphantly and congratulated each other on a job well done. The final tally indicated that we now had amassed canned hams, spam, beans, peaches, strawberries and ice cream. WOW, what a stash; all of the foodstuff needed to prevent this UDT detachment from possibly starving.

It wasn't long before we realized that the ice cream was quickly melting and we had to do something about it before it filled our berthing compartment with a creamy slush. To resolve this problem it was agreed that each man would dig in and do his best to consume as much ice cream as possible, including me. The mere thought of forcing myself to again eat a large amount of ice cream almost made me sick, afraid that I would soon feel like I did as a child when I over indulged. Nonetheless, along with every other man in our compartment, I ate ice cream until I could eat no more. We then moved to the fantail, or aft part of the ship, to toss overboard the evidence and all that couldn't be eaten. Reluctantly, we had eaten most of what we had taken so didn't actually waste that much. By evening, not a single man, involved in the ice cream caper, was eager for dinner. Most just stayed in the compartment trying to sleep off the ice cream binge they had been on earlier.

Then, later that night something totally unexpected happened. The five-gallon cans of peaches and strawberries started going off like cannons; their contents being blown all over everything and everyone in our sleeping compartment. The peaches and strawberries had been frozen and when they started to thaw, due to the heat in the compartment, the cans started to swell. When they reached their limit and could expand no further, they simply started to explode.

It was pandemonium until we finally came to the realization that the exploding cans weren't shells, fired by the Cubans, exploding in our compartment. However, until we came to this awareness, men were scurrying around, bumping into each other, and each man skating around the compartment, slipping and sliding, barely able to stay on his feet due to the massive amount of peaches and strawberries that covered the deck. It would have been a different matter if only the deck had been covered but this wasn't the case. I don't think there was a square inch of our compartment that hadn't been saturated with this sticky substance. The bulkheads (walls) the overhead (ceiling) our racks (beds) including mattresses and mattress covers, all of our clothing and swim gear, everything was covered with peaches and strawberries. And to top it off, each and every man was covered from head to toe with this sticky mess that was now starting to dry fast and harden.

The Officers and Chief Petty Officers assigned to the UDT Detachment did not berth in the same compartment as the enlisted men but it wasn't long before they found out what had happened. While they were not happy with what we had done, they nonetheless came to our aid. You may ask why, but that is the way of the Teams, Officers and enlisted men stick together. As part of a plea bargaining agreement, they struck with the ship's Captain; we were required to return what was left of our stash to the ship's pantry. We would then spend the remainder of that night and the better part of the following day cleaning up the mess we had caused. For what we had done there could have been severe penalties but we had gotten off easy and we knew it.

As it turned out, it was no easy matter cleaning up all of the now dried peaches and strawberries. To do this we were required to use salt water because fresh water is a coveted commodity aboard ship and always in short supply. Part of the problem was that soap and salt water don't work that well together. This would make the job much more difficult but after many long hours of hard work we did eventually complete the task. After cleaning the compartment we turned to the more difficult aspect of this whole process, that of washing our clothes and swim gear in salt water. Eventually we did reach the point that our clothing and gear was no longer sticky. As for our bodies, salt water baths are never fun but this is something we had done before and would certainly do many more times; besides, we were just lucky not to have received harsher punishments.

27. BEARTRACKS AND THE PILOT

One truly remarkable frogman was an individual that went by the rather unusual name of "Beartracks;" but for short, his fellow Teammates affectionately called him "Tracks." His real name was A.D. Allen and he was a Shipfitter First Class during the early to mid-1960's when he was assigned to UDT-12. Now there could be a number of reasons that you might call someone Beartracks, but as you probably have already guessed, the man had huge feet. His feet were long and wide and when he walked barefoot in the sand the print he left looked like it might have come from a huge bear. Tracks stood probably 6'6" tall and weighed close to two hundred fifty pounds. So, as you can see, there was more big to Tracks than just his feet. His most remarkable attribute had nothing to do with his shoe size, height, or weight, but instead would have to be credited to his strength. Tracks was probably the strongest man in the Teams and as far as I can remember, the strongest man I have ever met. What was most unusual about Tracks was the fact that his strength didn't come from constantly lifting weights, or from performing any other manner of strength related exercises, strong just happened to be something that made up his being.

Tracks didn't flaunt his strength nor was he a bully; quite the contrary, he was an individual that didn't raise his voice or push people around. He was quiet, well liked by all of his Teammates and pretty much stayed to himself. Usually, when you saw him around the Team Compound he would have a smoking pipe in his right hand and a smile on his face. He was a person who took what life had to give him and never seemed to let things get him down.

Tracks was in charge of the Team Dive Locker and as such was responsible for maintaining and charging UDT-12 rigs for both air and mixed gas diving. In addition to this primary assignment, and because of his extraordinary strength, Tracks was often times the assigned pick-up or sling man on operations that required swimmer recovery. Having completed a beach reconnaissance the swimmers would swim to a designated location. Tracks would then take up his sling man position in an Inflatable Boat Small (IBS), which was attached to the seaward side of the Landing Craft Personnel Recovery (LCPR), more commonly referred to as the pick-up boat. The swimmers would then form a straight line horizontal to the beach, maintaining a distance of roughly twenty-five feet between each man. As the boat came down the line of swimmers, each man would kick as hard as possible to propel his upper torso out of the water. Then, once the swimmers arm was in the sling the pick-up man would pull the swimmer into the IBS and the man would then scramble over the gunnels and into the LCPR.

For most sling men, even the strongest, this was a two-man operation. Once the swimmers arm was in the sling and the sling man started to pull the swimmer out of the water and up into the IBS, a second man in the IBS would grab hold of the swimmer and pull him over the side. While this was the normal procedure, it did not apply to Beartracks. When Tracks was the sling man, even if the swimmer had not kicked hard enough to get his upper torso out of the water; once he grabbled the sling, Tracks would propel the swimmer with such force that the man came out of the water and into the boat like he had been shot out of a cannon. When Tracks was the sling man, it was assured that you were going to get a ride. Let me just say that if this were something that Disneyland had to offer, it would have surely been an E-ticket ride. In his capacity as sling man, Tracks was unparalleled, he stood above all others.

While there are many more stories that I could attribute to Tracks, they would mostly be from second hand sources, stories that I heard but didn't witness.

However, there was an incident that I did witness and I will share that story with you now. This should give you a better understanding of the strength of this gentle giant.

During the Cuban Missile Crises, the ship to which our UDT-12 Detachment was assigned had been charged with the task, along with other Navy ships, to quarantine or blockade the water around Cuba. We were to prevent Russian ships from delivering their cargo of missiles to Cuban ports. After several days of maintaining this blockade, our ship was relieved and ordered to steam to the U.S. Naval Base, which is located in Guantonimo Bay, Cuba. Before we were to make our way to the Naval Base we were ordered to come along side a Navy Aircraft Carrier to accept the high line transfer of a Navy pilot. The pilot had been severely injured when his plan crashed into the flight deck of the carrier as he attempted a landing during heavy seas.

High lining is a maneuver that every ship's crew practices over and over again and though difficult it can be easily accomplished by veteran Captains of all Naval Vessels. When two ships pull along side each other a line or rope is shot across from one ship to the other. The line is then secured to a heavier line that is then pulled across to the opposite ship. Once this has been accomplished, several more lines are transferred from one ship to the other and once done you can move mail, cargo, food, fuel lines, or whatever it is you desire to move, even human cargo from one ship to the other. In this case we were to receive the pilot and once on board, transfer him to the Naval Base at Guantonimo. From there he would be flown back to the Continental United States and a hospital that could provide adequate care.

The transfer went smoothly and soon we were on our way to the Naval Base. When we arrived we pulled alongside the only pier at the Base and after securing the ship we were asked to bring the Navy

Pilot topside so he could be placed in an ambulance and moved to a waiting plane at the base airfield. Moving the pilot turned out to be no easy task. The man had been placed in a full body cast and he was resting in the metal and mesh sling that was used to high line him from the Aircraft Carrier to our ship. It took four of us to lift and move the man up the passageway and onto the fantail or aft section of the ship. When I say the man was covered in a full body cast I mean he was completely covered in plaster. From the top of his head to the bottom of his feet he was incased in plaster. Only his eyes nose and mouth were not covered and in the heat of this temperate climate, plus all of the injuries he had sustained, I can only imagine how uncomfortable the man must have been. After a several minute break, the four of us once again lifted the litter but were unable to walk it down the gangplank and onto the pier; the gangplank was just too narrow. By this time, Beartracks was standing on the pier and told us to lift the litter and man over the side of the ship to him. We knew this wasn't a good idea; after all it was all that the four of us could do to lift the litter. If we could hand the litter to Tracks it could only be done with considerable difficulty. Tracks told us to quit wasting time and hand him the pilot, so we did. Tracks simply reached out both arms and we struggled to set the litter, pilot and all, in Tracks outstretched arms. You could hear mumbling from the pilot but I couldn't distinguish his words and could only imagine what he was trying to say. What I did notice were his eyes, they were wide open and appeared bigger than the two holes that had been cut in his cast and they appeared to be panic-stricken.

    As I stood there and looked at Tracks all I could think was what a remarkable and powerful person he is. It simply looked like Tracks was cradling a small baby; he made it look so easy. Tracks then turned around and walked with the pilot approximately fifty feet to where the ambulance waited and placed the litter inside. The two ambulance attendants looked on in astonishment but said nothing. Tracks then took out his pipe, light it and walked back to the ship as though nothing had happened.

    Beartracks will forever be remembered by his Teammates and I am sure each could tell a different story about this gentle giant. As for me, I will always remember how easily Tracks handled the pilot, what he did seemed so effortless. The one thing I have often wondered, did the pilot recover from the damage inflicted by that uneventful landing. Also, I can't help but wonder what he thought about Beartracks, this man who so casually and easily took responsibility of the situation that day when he was young and in the Navy.

28. TRIUMPH MOTORCYCLES

Triumph, oh what a word. While it stands for victory, achievement, success, and accomplishment, it also stands for motorcycle. And for me the two words, "Triumph" and "Motorcycle" are synonymous with a man I served with during BUDS Training and then UDT-12. In fact, we even served together for one year on the USS *Saint Paul* before we were dispatched to BUDS Training. His name is Mike Paul, and today, even after forty years, just thinking of Mike floods my mind with many fond memories.

Mike was a Navy Lieutenant and graduate of the United States Naval Academy. He was born and raised in Washington State, but I know little of his life before I met him in the Navy. I am sure he had loving parents, as is the case with most of us, but God only knows how they survived his high school years. That is, assuming he was as wild then as he was during the years I knew him. I only say this because Mike was capable of raising more hell than any three normal people and guaranteed, wherever Mike was, action ensued. Although he was highly intelligent, Mike lacked common sense, or maybe it was just his way of going against the grain, or what most people consider normal. Whatever the situation, he was fun to be around and like I said, where Mike was, action was guaranteed.

Shortly after BUDS Training and our assignment to UDT-12, Mike's antics, which involved an old Model-T Ford, caught the attention of the Commanding Officer (C.O.) of the Naval Amphibious Base where we were stationed. In his Model-T, Mike would speed through the front gate (run the gate) of the Amphibious Base without stopping, or even slowing down for that matter. The Shore Patrol (S.P.), whose job it was to check everyone entering the base, would then have to dispatch a Jeep to chase him down. Having done this on more than one occasion and for numerous other driving infractions, Mike's driving privileges were revoked, and his car banned from the Amphibious Base, as well as Coronado. This is the subject of another story, so I won't go into the details now. Things grew worse as Mr. Paul continued to harass the Base C.O. Mike apparently enjoyed getting under this man's skin, and he did that extremely well. Eventually, he was assigned to oversee a detachment of men from UDT-12 and sent to Cuba. This occurred at the time of the Cuban Missile Crisis and was intended to remove Mike from the limelight, while giving the Base Commander a chance to cool off.

Three months passed, President Kennedy averted World War III with the Russians, and Mike Paul, with his detachment of Frogmen, returned to Coronado. We arrived shortly before Christmas and were elated to be back home and reunited with our families and friends. As for Mr. Paul, he took an extended leave to spend the holiday season with his family. We all enjoyed a marvelous Christmas, a Happy New Year, and I anxiously waited to see what 1963 had in store for us.

Then, about the middle of January, Mike Paul returned. Happy to be back, Mike was well rested and ready to go. The morning passed without incident and shortly after lunch, Jim Foley, another member of Team-12, and I went for a run down the Strand toward Imperial Beach. This was what I loved most about being in the Teams, the freedom to run, swim, lift weights, and exercise all day every day. I could never quite get over the fact that I was being paid to do all the things I loved most in life. Yes indeed, what more could a man ask.

On the return leg of our run, I could see what appeared to be a motorcycle coming toward us. As the figure on the bike drew nearer, I could see that it was Mr. Paul. He was weaving back and forth, from the sandy beach at the ocean's edge and then out into the ocean and then back to the sand, screaming and laughing all the while. He raced past us, spun around, and with the bike at full throttle, veered into the ocean as he passed us the second time. This time, however, a wave broke right in front of the bike, stopping his forward progress as assuredly as if he had hit a brick wall. Mike, in turn, flew over the handlebars, landing approximately thirty feet in front of the bike. Still screaming and laughing, Mike picked himself up, looked at the two of us, and shouted, "HOOYAH, what a ride!" Without saying a word to each other, both Jim and I knew that the quiet times, experienced while Mr. Paul was on leave, were a thing of the past.

We helped Mr. Paul retrieve his mighty Triumph from the ocean, but no matter how hard we tried, we could not restart it. The saltwater had fouled the ignition, so we wound up taking turns pushing the bike back to the Team compound. On the way back, Mike explained to us the "Mike Paul Philosophy" regarding restricted driving. Simply stated, while he was not allowed to bring a car onto the base, or into Coronado, no one had said anything about a motorcycle. Mike was being Mike, and he was convinced that he had figured out a way to circumvent the system. At the Team Compound, we flushed out the saltwater and sand with freshwater, used an air hose to blow away the freshwater, dried out the electrical system, and the bike fired up, good as new.

It was late afternoon when Jim and I finished working out, showered, put on our fatigues, and started to walk across the highway to the Amphibious Base for dinner. I should explain that the Team Compound is located on the Strand, south of Coronado, very close to the beautiful Pacific Ocean. A highway that runs from Coronado to Imperial Beach separates the Team Compound from the Amphibious Base where our barracks was located. The Base also has a Theatre, Mess Hall, Post Office, and other amenities that are intended for both Team and Base personnel. However, the Team Compound is isolated from the Amphibious Base and while Team members have access to the Base, Base personnel do not have access to the Team Compound.

As we left the compound and started across the highway, Mr. Paul came riding up to us on his Triumph. There he was, smiling like the proverbial cat, and there his bike was shining like a diamond. This would be the first time for Mike to take his bike onto the base, and he wanted to make it a memorable occasion. With that, he told us to hop on so we could share in the moment. Knowing there wasn't room for both of us, we laughed and continued walking. Mike pulled along side of us and said, "Come on, both of you get on, don't keep me waiting, let's go, let's go." At that, Jim and I climbed on behind Mike, or I should say squeezed on behind Mike, and we were underway.

The ride from the Team Compound to the front gate is relatively short, no more than two to three hundred yards. As we neared the gate, the Shore Patrol stepped in front of Mike, thinking he would stop, but that was a mistake. Mike raced by, nearly knocking him over. Chasing us on foot, blowing his whistle, and shouting obscenities, the S.P. was no match for Mr. Paul. Then, a second S.P., this time in a Jeep, joined in the chase. Lights flashing, siren blaring, the pursuit was on, and this made Mike as happy as a kid in a candy store. Mike dropped us off at the mess hall, waited until the Jeep drew near, and then took off once again to give his pursuer a tour of the base. As we stood in front of the mess hall, we could hear the sound of the Jeep's siren as the chase went from one side of the base to the other. Then Mike passed us once again, laughing and waving as he raced toward the front gate and freedom. He raced past the S.P. as he exited the base and then turned south toward Imperial Beach. The chase ended at that point, so Jim and I went in to eat our dinner. One thing for certain, Mr. Paul was definitely back.

Mike returned from Imperial Beach late that night and parked his bike in the Team Compound. The word of what had happened was circulating like wild fire, and this only added to Mike's jubilation. Because of our uniforms, the S.P. knew it was someone from the Teams who had run the gate, but at that time, they still didn't know who it was. I am sure the Base C.O. had a good idea who the culprit might be, and I had to laugh when I thought about that. Mike was up to his old tricks once more.

Several days passed before I saw "Team Triumph" once again. This time, Mike was chasing a young woman thru a park in Coronado. Dogs weren't allowed in the park, let alone motorcycles, but there was Mike in all his glory. The park was across from, and one block east, of the Coronado Police Department but this did nothing to dissuade Mike from his pursuit of the young woman. All the while the chase ensued, she was screaming loud enough to wake the dead. When Mike saw me, he waved and then continued his chase. One of the police officers heard all the commotion and came out to see what was happening. When he ran across the street, Mike laughed, discontinued the chase, and headed south once again to Imperial Beach. Soon, several police cruisers were headed in that direction, but Mike had too much of a lead by that time, and I knew he wouldn't be caught.

Mike was to make several more runs on the main gate of the Amphibious Base before he was finally captured. Then, as with his Model-T, Mike's Triumph Motorcycle was banned from the Amphibious Base, as well as from Coronado. Once again, Mike had fallen victim to the power of the Base Commanding Officer. Surprisingly, no major punishment was invoked for Mike's actions but, as you might guess, Mike felt the loss of his motorcycle to be excessive. The Commanding Officer of UDT-12 didn't get too worked up over the whole matter because actions such as these are more readily accepted in the Teams. Punishment in the Teams is usually reserved for gross negligence or doing something that negatively impacts another's life and this didn't seem to meet either of those criteria.

29. THE SILVER STRAND

A link that connects Coronado to Imperial Beach and San Diego, the Silver Strand is a beautiful stretch of sand, which separates the Pacific Ocean from the San Diego Bay. It also serves as a secondary link to San Diego, thru the use of a highway that runs its length. The primary link, between San Diego and Coronado, is the Coronado Bay Bridge, which was erected in the latter part of the nineteen sixties. Before the bridge was built, the only other way to reach Coronado was via the Coronado Ferry. The ferryboat ride provided direct access from downtown San Diego to Coronado and was a relaxing, peaceful, and fun way of traveling between these two cities.

Coronado is a quaint community that is home to both an upper class civilian community and several important Naval installations. While Coronado serves as the homeport for various Naval ships, it is also home to the Naval Amphibious Base and the North Island Naval Air Station. The Navy's UDT/SEAL Teams, as well as Basic Underwater Demolition SEAL Training (BUDS) also call Coronado home. So, as you can see, Coronado is a rather diverse community, comprised of both a military and civilian population who get along quite amicably.

Now, as I think back on my time in the Teams, I can recall many stories that are related to the Silver Strand. While going thru BUDS, we spent long hours training on and along the Strand, as well as in the ocean and bay that it separated. After training, the Strand served as our link to Imperial Beach for parties and to San Diego when we couldn't afford the ferryboat ride. This was the early nineteen sixties, gas was cheep, and the Strand also provided a direct link to Tijuana and all that Mexico had to offer. The Strand provided miles of sand for running and training, while the highway that ran its length was often used to test who had the fastest car. Yes, the Strand was used by all of us, who served in the Teams, for various reasons and thus there are numerous stories that relate to this stretch of sand. However, there is one story that always comes to mind when I think of the Silver Strand.

    Gary Lanphier, Bob Wagner, and I had been members of Class-28 and graduated to the Teams in July 1962. We had developed our friendship during BUDS and remained friends after training, although our Team assignments varied and took us in different directions. It was January 1963, and I had recently returned from Cuba, and Bob had just returned from Viet Nam. Gary and I were anxious to see him and catch up on all that had happened since we were last together. These are the times in the Teams that you cherish, a time to renew friendships, a time to get away from it all and raise a little hell, a time to laugh and catch up.

    Bob was a huge man. He was built and looked quite a bit like Arnold Schwarzenegger, although no one knew who Arnold was at that time. Bob had been a heavyweight boxer and was the one man you would want to cover your back in a street fight, or for that matter, at any time trouble broke out. Gary, on the other hand, was of average height and build, but Gary could fool you. Not that much to look at, Gary came to be one of the toughest men in the Teams and one of the toughest men I have ever known. But the main point I want to make here is that we were friends and happy for the opportunity to be together once again.

    Bob's flight from Viet Nam terminated at the Naval Air Station on Coronado Island, and he arrived in the Team Compound at about the same time we fell in for muster, at zero seven hundred hours, or seven a.m. He was still wearing his jungle fatigues so after showering and changing into a clean uniform, he sat down outside and started lacing up his boots. At this time, Gary walked over to Bob and stepped on the top of Bob's spit-shined jump boots. Don't ask me why; he just did it and walked away. Bob looked irritated; I looked surprised, and Gary just laughed. Now, if you knew and understood Gary, you would know that this is his way of saying that he was happy to see you. This may sound a little strange but, nonetheless, this is Gary. When Bob didn't punish Gary for what he had done, Gary did it again. This time, however, when Gary raked the sole of his boot across the top of Bob's, Bob did take action. He grabbed Gary by the collar of his fatigue shirt, fell backward while inserting a foot in Gary's stomach, and threw him about ten feet thru the air. Gary landed with a huge thud, laughed, got up, brushed himself off, and then asked Bob if that was the best he had to offer. With that, we all laughed, greeted each other, and started to talk about all that had happened since we were last together.

Bob had been a member of one of the first SEAL Detachments deployed to Viet Nam, and what little he could tell us made it quite clear what awaited. He had returned with graphic pictures, taken after a "fire fight" at a Green Beret Fire Base that left a number of men dead and badly mangled. Although he wasn't able to go into great detail, he made it quite clear that a real shit storm loomed on the horizon.

The morning passed quickly, and Bob asked if we could take a ride with him down the Strand, to Imperial Beach (I.B.), for a beer. Because this was a reunion of sorts, our platoon leaders granted the request, and we were on our way. Bob's car had been dropped off several days before he returned from Viet Nam and he was anxious to get behind the wheel once again. I climbed into the backseat, Gary the front passenger seat, and with Bob behind the wheel, we were underway.

We left the Team Compound and as we laughed about times past, Bob settled in for the five minute run to I.B. Shortly into the trip, Gary made his move. With his left foot, he moved across the center strip and pushed down on the accelerator. Bob asked what he was doing, but Gary said nothing; he just sat there with this wicked smile on his face. I don't know how to explain it, other than to say it was a smile only Gary could produce and when he did, trouble awaited. Bob then hit Gary on the leg several times, but Gary just smiled and kept his foot on the accelerator. The car continued to gain speed, Gary smiled, I sat fixated in the backseat, and Bob smacked Gary on the back of his head. As I mentioned earlier, this was Gary. This was simply another way to let us know that he was happy to be with people he cared for and nothing more. That, however, didn't change the situation. By now, Bob's 1949 Ford was pushing forward, faster and faster, and there was no sign that Gary would concede to Bob's request that he remove his foot from the accelerator. Bob then gave Gary a shot to the head that would have put most men to sleep, but not Gary who just sat there with that same wicked smile on his face. Bob then hit Gary again and again. Gary's head bounced off of the passenger window and although blood was now flowing from Gary's nose and ears, he still refused to relinquish his control of the accelerator. It wasn't until Bob turned off the key in the ignition that Gary agreed to give in. By now, things had grown quiet, the car slowly rolled to a stop, Bob popped Gary several more times, for good measure, and Gary continued to smile. Soon after, we were all laughing once more, and Bob just sat there shaking his head. With that came Gary's concluding remark as he turned to the backseat and asked, "Isn't it great to be together again?"

    What happened that day might seem unusual to some who do not understand the way of men who served in the Teams. However, to men in the Teams, this story, maybe worthy of a laugh, wouldn't be considered that unusual. As for Gary, he was then as he is today, a man capable of taking extreme punishment, without displaying so much as a facial grimace. My friendship with Gary continues to this day, but sadly, not so with Bob who lost his life in 1968, while on a combat mission in Viet Nam. And, although he is no longer with us, there will always be a bond that binds the three of us, this fellowship of brothers that was forged long ago when we were young and in the Teams.

30. FASTER WASN'T NECESSARILY BETTER

During World War II, when members of the U.S. Navy's, Naval Combat Demolition Units (NCDU's) conducted reconnaissance missions and/or planted explosives on enemy held beaches, they encountered a serious problem when they swam out to sea for recovery or extraction. As the pick-up boat slowed to allow the swimmers to climb aboard, the boat, the crew, and the swimmers were exposed to shelling and small arms fire from the enemy who still controlled the beach. The pick-up boat and occupants were literally sitting ducks and easy prey for enemy sharp shooters. It didn't take long to realize that "a new recovery system had to be devised", one that would allow the pick-up boat to extract swimmers from the water without forcing the boat to slow down or stop.

It didn't take long for someone to come up with a solution. Basically, three components were needed to make this new pick-up possible and two of those components already existed. The first was the Landing Craft Personal Recovery (LCPR) or pick-up boat. The second component was the Inflatable Boat Small (IBS). The idea was to lash or secure the IBS to the port side of the LCPR. The port side of the boat always faces seaward during swimmer recovery. The third component of the equation was a new item called a pick-up sling. It would be the responsibility of one of the stronger Team members, kneeling inside the IBS, to snare each swimmer with this sling and pull him into the IBS.

With the new recovery system in place, the swimmers would swim out to the predetermined recovery area when their mission was complete. Once there, they would form a straight line horizontal to the beach, allowing a 25-foot separation between swimmers. The pick-up or sling man would then take up his position in the IBS. As the pick-up boat made its run down the line of swimmers; the sling man would pull the swimmers, one at a time, into the IBS. The swimmers would then scramble over the gunnels and into the LCPR.

To accomplish the actual swimmer pick-up, the man assigned this job uses a sling that is made of rubber, approximately the same diameter as a garden hose, and roughly three feet in circumference. As the boat makes its way down the line of swimmers, each swimmer holds up his arm, bent at the elbow, and is snared by the pick-up man who then pulls the swimmer into the IBS. In order to bring his body as far out of the water as possible, as the boat approaches, it is important for each swimmer to kick his legs as hard as he can. The swim fins propel the swimmer upward and, the further out of the water, the easier it is for the sling man to pull the swimmer into the IBS.

The most important aspect of the pick-up falls directly on the shoulders of the boat coxswain. A pick-up is only successful if all swimmers are snared on the first pass. If a swimmer is missed and the boat has to make a second run, the odds of losing the boat and all members of the operation, to enemy fire, is greatly enhanced. Therefore, it is the responsibility of the boat coxswain to maneuver the boat down the pick-up line, close enough to the swimmers so they may be snared, and at a speed that will allow each swimmer to be pulled into the IBS before the boat reaches the next swimmer. Timing, speed, and boat location are critical to the success of this operation.

So successful was this method of swimmer recovery during World War II, it was still being taught in Basic Underwater Demolition Seal (BUDS) when I went through training in 1962. As simple as it may sound, this is by no means an easy task for the swimmer, sling man, or boat coxswain to master. When we first learned this technique, many a trainee returned from these training exercises with black and blue bruises, covering the entire inside of his arm, caused by the impact of the pick-up sling.

While this had been an effective means of swimmer recovery, when using the slower, flat-bottomed boat, called Landing Craft Personal Recovery (LCPR), times were changing. During the early 1960's, new boats were making their way into the Teams. In 1963 we received much faster jet boats and with these new boats came the requirement to identify and implement a new swimmer recovery methodology. The hulls of these boats were constructed of fiberglass and two turbo-jet engines powered each boat. They could travel at speeds well in excess of 40 knots, easily three times faster than anything we had previously seen. These boats could sleep two crew members, had a small head forward, and an enclosed swimmer compartment that could accommodate as many as twenty swimmers, if an operation required a large contingent of operatives.

With this new boat, swimmer recovery took on a whole new meaning. When the boat made its first pass, two small swimmer recovery pods, connected by a long strand of nylon rope, would be dropped by the jet boat near the swimmers. Each pod was made of fiberglass and looked like the front section of a small rowboat that had been cut in half. The aft section of each pod was open and the pod was lined with a thin piece of foam rubber. Inside and along each side of the pod were three hand cutouts, one for each swimmer to hold onto, so he wouldn't slip out the back of the pod during recovery. Each pod was built to accommodate as many as six swimmers. The swimmers would first swim each recovery pod in opposite directions until the nylon rope that connected them became taut. With this accomplished, the swimmers would pull themselves into the pod, grab on tightly to their respective hand hold, then wait for the pick-up boat to make its second pass and winch them in.

The bow of the jet boat was equipped with a slightly bowed metal bar that extended down into the water. As the jet boat passed between the two pods, the nylon rope would pass up and over this piece of bowed metal and into a winch that was mounted on the bow of the boat. The two pods would then come together and be winched to the aft section of the boat. To complete the recovery operation, the swimmers would simply climb from the pod and enter the swimmer compartment. On paper, this is how it was intended to happen; but we were in for quite a surprise when we first attempted to implement this new method of swimmer recovery.

    I don't remember who coined the phrase, "peas in a pod", but that was the name attached to this new swimmer recovery technique; the swimmers were the peas. After a short stint in the classroom, we climbed aboard the new jet boats and headed to the Open Ocean for some practical application. Then, the first time we tried this pick-up procedure, it wasn't "peas in a pod" because none of us could hold on tightly enough; we were all ejected out the back of the pod. We treaded water and watched as the pods were winched up to the jet boat without a man inside. We had failed on our first try but were certain we would do better on the second attempt. With the jet boat going full throttle, we would attempt this several more times and each time experience the same result; no one could hold on tightly enough to remain within the pod.

    It was decided that the jet boat would slow down to half speed for the next try, but even at 20 knots, it was impossible for the swimmers to hold on. At 20 knots, we did remain in the pod for several seconds, and then experienced another anomaly. As the jet boat snatched the nylon line, the weight of the swimmers prevented the pods from moving forward until the nylon rope stretched to its limit and became taut. At that point we were treated to a sling shot ride that had to be similar to being catapulted from an aircraft carrier. Again, as the pods lurched forward, all of the swimmers were ejected out the back of the pod before anyone realized what had happened. After several more unsuccessful attempts we returned to the Team compound knowing that, like anything new, this was a learning experience and it could take a while to figure out the right way to tame this beast.

Back in the compound someone came up with the idea of adding a piece of looped nylon rope, that each swimmer could stick his hand through, and greatly enhance his chances of holding on. Drilling holes, near the existing swimmer handholds, and adding six looped pieces of nylon rope would accomplish this. Though we didn't know it at the time, this would create even more serious consequences.

The next day we were back in the ocean, confident that this newly added piece of nylon rope would solve the problem. For the first pass, only two swimmers would be in each of the pods and the jet boat would attempt the pick-up at half speed. The boat made its pass and even with two swimmers the nylon rope that separated the pods, had to stretch to its limit before the pods would once again lurch toward the pick-up boat. This time however, the nylon rope wrapped around the hand of one of the swimmers, stretched so tightly that when he was expelled out of the back of the pod he left most of the skin from his hand, still inside the pod, attached to the nylon rope. What had happened to the swimmer is similar to what happens when you apply the Chinese finger trap. In case you are not familiar with this device, I will explain. It is slightly larger in circumference than your index finger, roughly four inches long, and made of woven bamboo. When you insert a finger from each hand, into the device and pull outward, the bamboo stretches tightly around each finger. The harder you pull, the tighter the finger trap holds onto your fingers. You can't remove your fingers until you relax and push your fingers inward; this expands the size of the trap and allows you to gently remove one finger at a time. Apparently the nylon rope wrapped so tightly around the swimmers hand, that it reacted in a similar way as the Chinese finger trap. Something had to give and in this case it was the skin attached to the swimmers hand. Luckily his hand hadn't been severed. As for the other three swimmers, they suffered bruises and lacerations to the back of their hands, but nothing more serious. However, they too were expelled from their pods.

There would be a simple solution to this problem and it certainly wasn't the nylon hand loop. Through trial and error it was determined that the pick-up could be accomplished, if the jet boat slowed to 15 knots when it reached the nylon line that separated the two pods. The boat would maintain this speed until the two pods came together and the winching process had begun. This transpired within a 15 to 20 second time frame so it was determined that by doing this, little would be jeopardized. Once the winching process was successfully under way, the boat could then accelerate to full throttle without loosing any of the swimmers. In the Teams, few challenges would be met and resolved without personal sacrifice and this had been no exception. For every problem encountered in the Teams there was a solution and in this case, "faster wasn't necessarily better."

31. FRIENDSHIP CAME LATER

I don't know if it applies to others, but I have found that developing a friendship not only requires trust, honesty, hard work, and dedication, it also must withstand the test of time. Too many times I have found that friendships, easily formed, or those that happen during a first encounter, usually don't withstand any of the above tests, let alone the test of time. These friendships have ended, more often than not, even before I started to know that person. I think this has a lot to do with the fact that the person you first see and talk to does not always represent the person they actually are. After all, most of us show our better side during a first encounter to prevent the other person from seeing us as we really are.

On the other hand, I have found that many of the people I immediately disliked, from the moment I met them, have actually turned out to be those individuals who later became my best friends and whose friendships have withstood all steps leading up to and including the test of time. I think this is because in these instances, we both spoke what we honestly felt, we didn't withhold our feelings for fear of being thought of as less than the person we want that other person to think we are. Now, I know that what I have just written is by no means revolutionary, but it is important with regard to the story I am about to share with you.

It all started innocently enough in 1963 with a change in the command structure of Underwater Demolition Team 12 (UDT-12). At our morning muster, we were introduced to an officer who would assume the number-one position by becoming our new Team Captain. His name was William A. Robinson and his rank was that of Lieutenant Commander. He had most recently served in a fleet assignment but before that, he had completed BUDS Training and served in the Teams. Unlike enlisted men, career officers are required to rotate their Team assignment with one in the fleet if they plan to be promoted and make the Navy their career. If an officer is truly talented, and if returning to the Teams fits the future career plans of the officer and the Navy, then he may be offered a command position in the Teams, as was the case with Captain Robinson.

Our new Captain was not an easy man to read. His time in the Teams occurred long before I had arrived, so I knew nothing about him except what some of the other enlisted men, who did know him, could tell us, and that was very little. When he spoke to us, on that first morning, he made it quite clear that he was the man in charge. His junior line officers would continue to be responsible for the Platoons to which they were assigned and; therefore, any interaction between the men in these platoons and his office would come through them. This was in line with what had previously been the case; so basically, it would be business as usual.

Captain Robinson was of average height and build but, in the Teams, this meant little. Some of the smallest men in the Teams were the toughest, and I had learned that, like stated in the old maxim, you should never judge a book by its cover. What struck me about our new Captain was the fact that he seldom smiled. His basic demeanor was that of being very serious, even irritated.

The first Team meeting with our new Captain was uneventful due to the fact that it was an "all hands welcome aboard ceremony" and not individual or small group encounters. I was but one of approximately 90 enlisted men in Team-12, and it would be unlikely that I would ever have a personal meeting with our new Captain. That is, it would be unlikely that I would ever be called before him, as long as I did nothing serious enough to warrant his attention. I was just here to do my job, not to create problems, so I felt I had nothing to worry about. But, little did I know what fate had in store for me.

Several weeks passed and my only encounter with Captain Robinson would be the few times we passed each other in the Team compound, when he was on his way to the Strand for a swim or run. On these occasions he never spoke or smiled and it seemed that he was always deep in thought. He had not made any significant changes to the life we had known before his arrival, but he made certain that we knew that he expected each of us to be the best that we could be. To judge our performance, and to learn more about the men under his command, he found time to be a part of Team-12 training exercises, something our previous Captain, because of his demanding schedule, could not find time to do.

Now that Captain Robinson was settling into his new assignment, it was decided that an open house would be appropriate. This would give the Captain an opportunity to meet the men under his command and give us a chance to learn a little more about him. A Team-12 Officer, who lived in Coronado, offered his home for this event and both officers and enlisted men were invited.

I have never been one to enjoy an event such as this, so I decided not to attend. Before that evening would come to an end, I would wish that I had stuck to that decision. A Teammate and friend, Jim Foley, and I had gone to San Diego to a movie and dinner the evening of the open house. We returned to Coronado at about 9:30 p.m. and Jim suggested that we stop by the party to pay our respects and have a beer or two. Without much prodding, I agreed.

When we arrived the party was in full swing and the Coronado police had already come and gone several times. Team parties are usually more radical than most other parties and this was no exception. The home, where the party was held, was a handsome two-story structure with nice apportionments, very befitting a Team officer. Most of the enlisted men were on the second level, while the officers, including Captain Robinson, were gathered on the first floor. Jim and I waited for a break in the conversation at which time one of the officers introduced us to the Captain. We simply said hello, excused ourselves, and moved upstairs where the other enlisted men were raising hell and partying. Music was blaring, beer was flowing, and everyone was having a good time. These were all signs of a normal Team party and, as far as I could see, nothing too far removed from the normal.

Then it happened, something that I was totally unprepared for. As I turned my back and looked down where our Captain and the other officers were standing, one of my teammates dumped a pitcher of beer over the rail and directly on the Captain. By the time I realized what had happened all of the enlisted men, who had been standing beside me, had vanished into one of the rooms. There I was, standing by myself, with everyone on the first floor, including the Captain, looking up at me. The only thing you could hear was the music, not another sound was audible except for me trying to say that I didn't do it. I couldn't believe that I had let myself be put into this situation, but it was too late. The party took on a different demeanor and at this point, Jim and I decided it would be better if I got the hell out of there. As we passed, the Captain just stared, but said nothing. I tried again to say that I hadn't been the one to pour the beer, but this sounded very much like the empty words of a condemned man.

The rest of the weekend was uneventful, and all I could think about was what would happen on Monday when we all returned to the Team compound to start a new week. It didn't take long to find out when, shortly after our morning muster, I was ordered to the Captain's office. When given permission to enter, Captain Robinson was sitting behind his desk, mulling over some papers. After what seemed an eternity, he told me not to say a single word, but to listen carefully to what he had to say. Only after he had finished would I be allowed to speak, and what I had to say would be of extreme importance to my future well-being. He then went on to say, something to the effect, that I had disrespected him and in order to resolve this matter, I should meet him on the Strand, behind the Team compound, where he would commence to kick my ass. I stood frozen, unable to think, let alone speak, and could barely force myself to say that I was very sorry that this had happened, but would not fight him. I believe the Captain took what little I did say as an apology and then ordered me to leave his office. However, before I left, he said that in the future, it would be prudent of me to stay as far away from him as possible.

  From that day forward, I did as the Captain had suggested and always gave him plenty of room, on the few occasions our paths did cross, in and around the Team compound. He had never ordered any form of punishment for what he felt I had done and for that I was thankful. For the first week, my teammates would walk in the other direction whenever they saw me coming, but eventually life in the Teams started to work its way back to normal. In time, everyone had forgotten about the incident, everyone that is, except the Captain and me, or at least that is how I perceived it.

  As time passed, Captain Robinson's attitude toward me started to change. On the few occasions when we crossed each other's path, he would look at me and smile or say hello. The change was gradual, but it made me feel much better. Then, after my successful involvement with the *Mercury* Program, I felt that I had crossed the final hurdle and no longer felt anxious whenever the Captain came near. While he had not been involved in the decision to assign me to the "Astronaut Recovery Program," he did allow me to attend Jump School, at a time when this was considered a privilege and a choice opportunity sought by many.

Then, on one cold November night, I was assigned, along with eleven other men, to a night operation that could have easily cost my life and the lives of the other men involved. It was a submarine operation that would span two nights and require locking out of the submarine, swimming four miles to designated beaches, reconnoitering those beaches during the day, and then swimming four miles to the waiting submarine on the second night.

Due to a stupid mistake that cost me my wet suit, I was given the choice of making the return swim, without the wet suit, or becoming a prisoner and not completing the operation. I made the swim, which ultimately required us to spend five hours in the freezing waters of the Pacific Ocean before finally being picked-up by the submarine.

Having completed this difficult operation, we returned to our Team compound in Coronado to await the return of the other Team-12 members who were still conducting exercises related to the overall operation. Then, in a debriefing of the overall operation, conducted by Captain Robinson, the swimmers who had been assigned to the submarine operation were acknowledged for gathering relevant and meaningful data, as well as their unwavering commitment to duty. Captain Robinson then went on to say that he had spent roughly thirty minutes in the water checking obstacles that had been loaded with explosives for demolition. This occurred during another of the many operations conducted as a part of the overall exercise. He said that he was wearing a full wet suit, but no hood, and that before he had finished, he thought his ears had frozen. He then went on to say that he had no idea how Nickelson survived those five hours without a wet suit top and commented that he was proud to know me. He then walked to where I was sitting and shook my hand. Needless to say, I was overwhelmed by this gesture.

It had taken a very long time, but on that day, Captain Robinson and I became friends. A relationship that had started off in such a negative vein had, over time, developed into what would be a lasting friendship. Following this event, there would be many times when the Captain would call me into his office where we would talk about the Teams and events related to our lives in general. We would both leave the Teams in 1965, me to the life of a civilian and Captain Robinson to take on a new fleet assignment, another step up the ladder for this career officer. Sadly, Captain Robinson was killed some years later.

As it was with our Captain, so it is with many other men I knew in the Teams, and though we haven't seen each other for years, we will always be friends, and I will always look on them as if they were my brothers. However, the friendship that I shared with Captain Robinson will always mean more to me because it was a friendship that I would have never thought possible, a friendship that no one would have ever given a chance.

32. PROJECT *MERCURY: FAITH 7*

At twelve hundred hours, 16 May 1963, we boarded our helicopter and lifted into the air from the deck of the recovery ship, *U.S.S. Kearsarge*. We would remain there for the next thirty to forty-five minutes and then complete the task we had so thoroughly trained for. It would be our job to attach the flotation collar to Gordon Cooper's *Faith 7 Mercury Spacecraft* when it landed in the Pacific Ocean near Midway Island. We had prepared for this mission for the previous three months and anxiously awaited splashdown.

Then, over the headset came word that major problems had been encountered on board the Spacecraft. Apparently, Cooper had lost voice communication with the Cape and his on-board computer had failed. We were then informed that due to the magnitude of the problems, it would be highly unlikely that Cooper could land his spacecraft in the primary recovery area. We were ordered to remain airborne until the situation was fully understood. We were then told that we would be notified as soon as additional information was made available. At this point, it looked as though the spacecraft would splash down in a contingency area, perhaps several hundred miles from the primary landing area where we waited. In reality, the situation was critical. With no computer to signal the exact moment to fire his retro-rockets for reentry, and having no voice communication with the Cape, Cooper would have only his wristwatch to rely on. So precise was the timed firing of the retro-rockets, simply missing the mark by one second meant Cooper would overshoot the primary recovery area by one hundred miles. Two seconds, two hundred miles and so on until the cutoff point, ten seconds. At this time, his spacecraft would bounce off of the atmosphere and slingshot into space, never to return to Earth.

As we circled the *Kearsarge,* my mind went back over the events that led us to this particular moment in time. All members of the recovery team had been introduced to and spent time with Gordon Cooper at Cape Canaveral, while training for the recovery. We were there to demonstrate how adept we were in all matters related to Spacecraft Recovery Operations. Also, we would demonstrate how quickly and proficiently we could attach the flotation collar to his *Mercury Capsule* and then deal with simulated problems. In actuality, we were there to gain his trust.

Gordo, as he was more affectionately known, was a very amiable person and easy to be around. The day we placed the flotation collar on a mock-up capsule, in the ocean off of the Cape, Cooper paddled around the area in a one-man life raft, one used by downed pilots. He laughed and joked with us, as well as the many reporters that followed his every movement. This was the dawn of the space age, and the *Mercury* Astronauts were super stars. It seemed that America couldn't get enough of these men, and Cooper had no problem dealing with all of this newfound fame. We were told that Cooper was the most congenial of the *Mercury* Astronauts, and we certainly enjoyed the short time that we spent with him.

Men assigned to the "Astronaut Recovery Teams" (ART) were drawn from the ranks of "Underwater Demolition Teams" (UDT). The decision to use UDT was made following the loss of the second *Mercury Spacecraft, Liberty Bell 7,* after splashdown in the Pacific Ocean in July, 1961. The capsule's escape hatch had been blown prematurely, causing it to sink to the ocean's depths. NASA realized that this loss could have been prevented, had there been a flotation collar in place. They were, therefore, determined to prevent this from happening again and approached the Navy for help. Because of our familiarity with the water and adaptability when placed in adverse situations, men from UDT were obviously the best candidates for the job. That set the wheels in motion for what would follow.

Selection to one of the two Recovery Teams was quite another matter. This was considered a choice Temporary Duty Assignment and was eagerly sought after by practically every man in UDT-11 and 12. Once the initial three-man teams had been selected, those chosen were to continue in this assignment for the balance of the *Mercury Project's* remaining four flights. I wasn't one of the original candidates. In fact, I hadn't even started Basic Underwater Demolition SEAL Training (BUDS) when the original Astronaut Recovery Teams were selected in 1961. Then, when I graduated from BUDS in July 1962, only two flights remained: Wally Schirra's scheduled launch in October 1962, and Gordon Cooper's sixth and final *Mercury* flight planned for May 1963. From September thru December 1962, I was a member of a UDT Detachment deployed to Cuba as a result of the Cuban Missile Crisis.

Then, one morning in February 1963, the Executive Officer (XO) of UDT-12 addressed the Team at our morning muster. He stated that two men, previously assigned to the Astronaut Recovery Program, would be replaced. One was being reassigned and the other retiring. Two new candidates would fill these vacancies, one from Team-11, the second from Team-12. He asked for a show of hands, if anyone was interested in this assignment, and practically every man in Team-12 raised his hand. He then said that anyone wishing to do so should put his name on a piece of paper and drop it into a hat in the Team office. He would draw the name of the replacement at noon. After muster, there was a mad scramble to get in line and sign up for the noon drawing. I was probably the seventieth man in line; I looked at all of the men in front of me and measured the odds of my being selected. Not good, slim at best!

Having nothing to lose, and wanting this assignment, I stepped out of line, went to the XO's office, and knocked on his door. When given permission, I entered and asked him why he was choosing a replacement by drawing the name from a hat when I was obviously the man for the job. I went on to tell him that I would do a better job than any one standing in that long line and that he would be making a huge mistake if one of them were selected instead of me. He just sat there and listened intently. Then, a big smile came across his face, and he shook his head. Next came his response; "Nickelson, I like what you just did here the job is yours." With that, he confronted the men standing in line and announced that there would be no drawing; he had selected the replacement. Much to the chagrin of the other men, the job was mine. And that is how I came to be a member of the "Cooper Recovery Team."

For each *Mercury* recovery, there were two each three-man teams. The first, or primary recovery team, would be responsible for placing the flotation collar on the Spacecraft after splashdown. The secondary recovery team would serve as a backup; to replace the primary team should something unforeseen happen. Both teams are equally competent and as well trained, but only one would be designated as primary.

For the Cooper recovery, two men each from the existing recovery teams were assigned to the primary and secondary teams. With regard to the two new men, I would be assigned to one of the open slots, and the replacement from Team-11 the other. This would now be decided by the flip of a coin. The winner would be assigned to the primary team, which almost guaranteed hands-on participation. The loser would go to the secondary team, resigned to watch, unless something unforeseen happened. As luck would have it, I won the coin toss and the right to be a part of the Primary Recovery Team. Bob Allard, from Team-11, was assigned to the Secondary Recovery Team.

At that point, we were temporarily relieved of routine UDT duties and started training for the May 16, 1963, recovery. We worked with a replica of the *Mercury Capsule* and flotation collars provided to us by NASA. Two crews from Helicopter Anti-Submarine Squadron Six, the Navy's best, were teamed with us, and we worked closely together for the next several months. Two to four times a day, we would board the helicopter and fly to the replica capsule. We would then jump into the ocean and attach the flotation collar. We trained both day and night, in good weather and bad, until we could attach the collar blindfolded. NASA and the Navy Department also provided us with training manuals, covering every conceivable aspect of the mission, as well as pre-and post-recovery. We learned all features of the Spacecraft and how to treat an injured or unconscious astronaut. We learned how to safely blow the escape hatch, to remove an injured astronaut or, if uninjured and the astronaut simply chose to egress the spacecraft before it was hoisted aboard the recovery ship. This was a critical operation that involved explosives, and it had to be accomplished without hurting the Astronaut or tearing the flotation collar. In addition, we learned how to communicate with the recovery ship using various colored signal flares. Each flare had its own specific meaning and would be used if there were no other way to inform the helicopter or recovery ship of a distressful situation. While our primary role was to prevent the capsule from sinking, we were required to study the manuals until we understood every aspect of the mission. The training was thorough, exacting, and fun.

Then, a blast from my headset brought me back to the situation at hand. We were informed that it was still unknown whether we would be involved in the recovery. We were told that it was only seconds from impact time and again ordered to stand by and await further orders. Shortly after receiving this message, the improbable happened. Floating down under a bright red-and-white parachute was the *Faith 7 spacecraft* and Gordon Cooper. We were so close to the capsule, it seemed as though I could reach out and touch it. Gordon Cooper had done the impossible; he had maneuvered his *Faith 7 Spacecraft* to within four miles of the recovery ship. As hard to believe as it seemed, he had actually pulled it off. He had done this manually, with basically no help, other than his wristwatch.

We watched as the Spacecraft splashed down and waited for the parachute to separate from the craft before we made our move. The capsule lay on its side, while being dragged across the water by the parachute. Then, after several seconds, the parachute was released, and the capsule came to rest in its upright position. Within a matter of minutes, the helicopter was beside the *Faith 7 Capsule* and the recovery team, the three of us, were jumping from the helicopter and making our swim to the spacecraft. R.E. Sallient (our team leader) and I towed the flotation collar, while Bert Swift swam on ahead to assess the condition of Gordon Cooper. It took several minutes to reach the Capsule and then three to four minutes to install the flotation collar. All of our training had paid off; it went as smooth as glass.

Through a window, built into the side of the Spacecraft, we could see and communicate with Cooper. It was gratifying to know that the thirty-four hour, twenty-two orbit mission hadn't dampened his spirits. He was one very happy and relieved Astronaut. We then spent the next several minutes providing him with a status upgrade. We informed him of our position in relation to the ship, the condition of his craft, and asked him whether he wanted to egress now, or wait until he was lifted on board the *Kearsarge*. We then secured the capsule and, from underwater, took pictures of the heat shield, the metal and special alloy plate attached to the bottom of the spacecraft that prevented it from burning up on reentry.

A boat was dispatched from the *U.S.S. Kearsarge,* towing a long line (rope) that I attached to the Spacecraft. The capsule was then towed to the ship and hoisted aboard. Cooper had opted to remain inside the Capsule until he was safely on board the ship. The hatch was then blown and Cooper given a hero's welcome for his remarkable flight and unbelievable accomplishments. And so too, our job was now complete, we had done what we had been trained to do, and the Navy and Cooper were extremely satisfied with the support that we had provided.

Then, during our debriefing, one of the reporters asked if we were aware that a number of sharks had been swimming near the Capsule. None of us had seen the sharks, probably because we had been so focused on the job at hand. We were then asked what we would have done, had we known. To that, R.E. Sallient responded, "It would have been very crowded in that tiny Capsule, the three of us and Cooper."

Faith-7, Mercury capsule, with Gordon Cooper still inside the capsule. Nick Nickelson is hooking-up line to tow capsule back to ship.

U.S.S. *Kearsarge* in background. R.E. Sallient sitting on flotation collar, Nick Nickelson standing on collar, and Bert Swift is in the water. Gordon Cooper, inside capsule, awaits tow to ship.

Gordon Cooper stands in the center of picture wearing sunglasses. Standing on his right side is Leo Hamel, the Chief in charge of training both the primary and secondary recovery teams. Standing to Chief Hamel's right is the secondary recovery team (Allard, Whetzell, Allen) and to Gordon Cooper's left is the primary recovery team (Sallient, Swift, Nickelson - behind man with arm extended).

33. JUMP SCHOOL

It was 18 May 1963, and I had just returned to the Team Compound. For the previous three months, I had been on temporary duty, assigned to the Project *Mercury* Recovery Program. Several days earlier, we had placed the flotation collar on Gordon Cooper's *Faith-7 Mercury Capsule* after it had splashed down in the Pacific Ocean. Everything had gone well, and I had enjoyed this assignment, but was glad to be back in Coronado.

These were the Golden Days, not only for the UDT/SEAL Teams, but also for every man that served in the Teams. Every day, we were receiving and testing new and innovative equipment designed to make our lives better. There were new high-speed boats with fiberglass hulls, powered by twin turbo-jet engines. These boats could fly on water, but more importantly, they could fly on water while accommodating twenty swimmers in their crew compartments. These boats also required new and innovative swimmer pick-up techniques, because of their greatly increased speed. For diving, new Mark-Five, semi-closed re-breathers had burst onto the scene, allowing deeper dives and stealthier swimmer sneak attacks but requiring mixed gases. Then, the new M-14, full automatic rifle, had set new standards as a tool for the Teams. There was a new handheld sonar device, an innovative underwater tool used in search and recovery. And, this is just a small sample of the equipment making its way into the Teams during the early nineteen sixties. All of this equipment would require thorough and arduous testing before it could become permanently incorporated into the Teams. That meant many long man-hours and the dedication of every man. This was a new beginning, the start of revolutionary and revitalized UDT/SEAL Teams, and I was proud to be a part of this effort.

In addition to equipment, billets were becoming available for Jump School. Prior to 1963, few men in the Teams were jump qualified, but this was about to change. Parachuting was now viewed as a viable tool, well suited for use by the Teams, as a method of insertion into a combat area. Prior to this time, it had been too expensive for the Teams to send men to jump school. There were isolated instances where men were able to earn their wings, but now money was becoming available for large numbers of Team members to attend the Army's jump school at Fort Benning, Georgia.

In May 1963, UDT-12 was allocated ten billets for the June program at Benning. This was an opportunity to get my wings, and I wanted to be one of those selected. When called to the Captain's office, I was certain that it was for that reason and prematurely thanked him for allowing me this opportunity. He told me to sit down, that I hadn't been called in because of jump school. Before he stated the reason for my being there, I was reminded that I had recently returned from the *Mercury* Recovery Program, a choice assignment, and that other men should be given the opportunity to attend jump school. He then went on to tell me why I had been called to his office. Apparently, the Mayor of Colorado Springs, my hometown before I joined the Navy, had called to ask if I might be allowed to return home for a parade. The parade would be given to honor Gordon Cooper for his historic *Mercury* space flight. Because I had been a member of the three-man recovery team and because Colorado Springs was my hometown, the Mayor felt that it was appropriate for me to be there as well. The Captain went on to say that this would be a good opportunity to gain positive press for the Teams and asked what I thought. When I didn't respond immediately, he made a fatal mistake. He asked what would I rather do, go to Georgia and jump school, during the hottest part of summer, or Colorado, my hometown, family, and all the glory and festivities that accompany a parade. From the way the Captain had presented it, I knew that he felt I would opt for the parade. He had barely finished speaking when I gave him my answer: "Jump School!" I then added that if he allowed me to attend jump school, I would bring home the class honor-man trophy. His response was exactly what I had hoped to hear; "I can't believe that you would rather suffer through the Georgia heat than attend the festivities in Colorado, but I did give you a choice." He then looked at me, shook his head, and said, "You have my permission to attend jump school; now get the hell out of here."

The typical jump school program at Fort Benning lasts four weeks. The first week is to condition the candidates and prepare them physically for the real training that would follow. Because men in the Teams are always in excellent condition, they are not required to complete the first week of training. It had been pre-arranged that we would be joining a class comprised of roughly two hundred men. While the majority of trainees in our class were from the Army, there were several men from the Marine Corp, as well as a small number of men from the Air Force Academy.

Our flight was scheduled to depart from San Diego at the end of May. There would be a total of twenty men, ten each from Teams Eleven and Twelve, scheduled to attend this session. We would join our class and begin training on the first of June. When we arrived, the officers were sent to the officers' quarters, and the enlisted men moved into barracks occupied by Army enlisted men. B.T. Russell (B.T.), also from Team-12 and a good friend, and I were assigned to a room that we would share for the next three weeks. In addition, there was a kitten that came with the room. Although she was very small, the kitten made it quite clear that the room belonged to her, and we were only guests. This little lady would provide many nights filled with laughter before we were to complete training and return to Coronado. She had no idea how much fun she would bring into our lives.

Compared to Basic Underwater Demolition SEAL Training (BUDS), Jump School was a piece of cake. It isn't my intention to demean this fine Army program, but it just wasn't that difficult. The Army required that we all had our heads shaved and for me that was the most difficult part of the program. In addition to having my head shaved, I didn't care for getting up at four-thirty in the morning. Other than that, I enjoyed jump school and intended to make the best of this opportunity.

The first week of training required that we become familiar with the main and reserve parachutes. We practiced proper deployment and jump techniques from mock planes that served as trainers. We learned the fundamentals of landing properly called the "Parachute Landing Fall" (PLF). We practiced releasing the parachute while being dragged along by the wind having successfully landed on the ground. In addition, we were required to do considerable Physical Training (P.T.) and running. Mostly, it was interesting and fun.

At the end of our first week of training, the Instructors announced that I had been selected as that week's honor-man. I was then given a white helmet that signifies this honor. In addition, I was handed the class flag and placed roughly ten paces in front of the class. I was to lead them as we marched back to our barracks. About halfway to the barracks, things became very quiet. When I couldn't stand the silence any longer, I turned around to find no one there. The class had taken a right turn some time back and left me all alone and looking stupid. There I was in a white helmet, carrying a flag, the leader of a band that had deserted. When I did make it back to the barracks, everyone had a good laugh and though embarrassed, I had to laugh as well.

Georgia, during the month of June, is extremely hot and humid and coming from California, it took us a while to acclimate to those conditions. The nights were as hot as the days and after taking a shower, toweling off, and dressing, you were as wet from perspiration as you were right after stepping out of the shower. There was never a breeze to cool things off, so we did the best we could to forget the heat. Now, this is where our kitten comes in.

One night as we lay on our bunks and the kitten played on the floor, a huge cockroach entered our room. B.T. and I looked at it, then at each other, and then B.T. picked up the kitten. I had never seen a cockroach this large; it had to have been the size of a silver dollar, but longer than big around. It didn't move fast, but rather strolled along the floor as if it were looking for a fight. Then, when the kitten realized that her territory had been compromised, she decided it was time to take action. She squirmed and squealed until B.T. finally let her go. Now it was her turn to show us what she was made of. She immediately leapt from the bunk, her two front paws landing directly on the back of the cockroach. Time stood still as she stood there victorious, having pinned the enemy to the floor. About the time she looked back at us for our approval, it happened. The cockroach simply started walking away with the kitten's front paws still on its back. The kitten couldn't believe what was happening, but refused to surrender control. Her front and rear paws grew farther apart until she lost her balance and fell flat on her chin. Not wanting to be humiliated by this cockroach invader, the kitten jumped into the air, this time landing with all fours on the back of the enemy. Once again, she looked back for our approval and then tried to bite thru the heavy armor of this adversary. No good, it was too thick for the kitten's teeth, nothing happened. The kitten then jumped again and again into the air, each time landing with her front paws on the back of the cockroach. Between each jump, the cockroach inched its way back toward the door through which it had entered. I wouldn't have wanted to tell the kitten, but when the cockroach crawled back under the door, I would have declared it the winner. Not as far as the kitten was concerned and she triumphantly ran back over and jumped up on B.T.'s bunk, seeking his approval. She knew she had defeated the evil invader. This wasn't the end; our little lady would provide many more laughs before our time at Benning would come to an end.

    The third week of jump school (our second) was much more interesting. We started to jump from the tower, and we were also exposed to the parachute drop. The tower stood about three stories above the ground and was equipped with lines that ran about one hundred yards away from the tower, gradually ending at a small raised spot, something like a hill. Each trainee would hook his parachute harness to this line, then jump from the door, just as if he were jumping from an airplane. He would then slide down the line to the hill. The parachute drop was rather like a ride at Knott's Berry Farm, an amusement park in Anaheim, California. The main difference is that you are in a parachute harness that is rigged to a parachute. Also the tower extends higher into the air than the one at Knott's. After being hoisted to the apex of the parachute tower, then dropped, you floated slowly to the ground. You are then judged on how well you execute a Parachute Landing Fall, (PLF). After mastering the parachute drop, more time was spent jumping from the tower. This time, however, we were to act out a situation in which our main chute didn't deploy, and we were to go thru the routine of shaking out our reserve chute. The reserve chute is pulled from a small pack, located below your waist, and is always deployed by hand.

    Then came the final week and five parachute jumps from an airplane. By this time, we were anxious and ready to make a real jump. The plan was to make one jump a day for five days. Then, after the fifth and final jump, we would be given our jump wings. When Monday arrived, it started to rain. The rain was a welcome relief but why now; this was interfering with our jump schedule. Tuesday then Wednesday and the rain continued to fall. We all wondered if this meant that we would be held over to make up the missed jumps the following week. Then Thursday, sunshine and wind and we were off to the awaiting planes. We were now scheduled to make two jumps on Thursday and three on Friday. The wind was blowing hard as we boarded the airplane for our first jump. This didn't mean anything to us; we were just happy that we could finally put into practice all that we had been taught.

Our class was one of probably ten classes going through training at that particular time. Therefore, there must have been twenty planes filled with trainees lifting off of the ground and flying toward the Drop Zone (DZ). Anxiety built as we grew closer to the DZ; then the green light came on, and we were ordered to "Stand-up, hook-up, shuffle to the door." Then the command, "Go" and each man started to shuffle toward the open door and his first leap into the wild blue. All I could think about, once I realized the chute had opened, was what a great sensation and how beautiful it was floating down to the ground. I felt like a feather. Then, when I saw the ground rushing up to meet me, my thoughts turned back to making a perfect PLF when I landed. The wind had caused me to oscillate back and forth, but I didn't expect the reaction that would soon follow. When I landed, my feet first hit the ground and then my head. This wasn't the way it was supposed to happen and for several seconds, I thought I was dead. A perfect PLF requires that first your feet touch the ground and then your calf, thigh, side, and you roll over on your back. Your head isn't an extremity that is supposed enter into the equation. When the bells stopped ringing, I recovered and rolled up my chute. As I walked to the truck that would return us to the base, all I could think about was the four remaining jumps. If they were to be like this one, I would be returning to Coronado in a box.

We returned to the hanger area and were immediately given freshly packed parachutes and marched out to the waiting planes. I was feeling much better and knew that this next jump would come with a softer landing. I was told to reach up and pull down hard on my risers, the lines that go from the parachute harness to the parachute, and then let go. Doing this several times would stop the oscillation. I was now well prepared and as I drifted toward the ground, did as I had been told. The landing was similar to the first except I didn't think I was dead this time. Again, I rolled up my parachute, and we returned to the base. It was a restless night's sleep, as I thought about the remaining three jumps that would follow on Friday.

Friday morning arrived, and my third jump went pretty well. The wind wasn't blowing quite as hard, and this time I pulled the risers down to my foot, placed my boot in the risers, and pushed down as hard as I could before letting go. This did much to thwart the oscillation. Cool, this new risers to foot worked pretty well, and the fourth jump went smoothly. Then, on our fifth and final jump, the sergeant in charge ordered all of the men wearing white helmets to follow him. In my wildest dreams, I couldn't have imagined what would follow. At the hanger, we were informed that we would jump with an equipment pack. Now an equipment pack stands about three feet tall and weighs approximately one hundred pounds. It is attached to a twenty-foot lanyard that is attached to you. You place the equipment pack on the top of your boots and once you jump from the plane, the pack drops below you and precedes you to the ground, pulling you all the way.

All I could think about was dying, on this my final jump.

With help, I made it into the plane and sat down. Some of my Teammates were having a real laugh as I sat there, my life flashing before my eyes. I would have been a whole lot happier to be anywhere else at that time. Then, the green light came on, and I was standing in the door. I closed my eyes and jumped, the chute opened and as I looked down, I could see the equipment bag dangling below me. It seemed as though I was falling twice as fast as the other men, but I think that was my mind playing tricks on me. Then I could see the ground racing toward me and before I realized what had happened, I was standing on the ground. I was still alive and it was as if I had stepped off of a coffee table. An Instructor was madly blowing his whistle and telling me to do a PLF. Because I was so excited, I had forgotten, but then did as directed. I wasn't dead; I wasn't even hurt; I was fine, and I had truly enjoyed this final jump. What an adventure this had been, but thankfully it was over. We were then given our jump wings right there on the Drop Zone. We had successfully completed jump school and made the prescribed five parachute jumps.

After the graduation ceremony, we returned to our barracks, packed, and said goodbye to the men we had met and befriended. For B.T. and me, the hardest goodbye we would make would be to the kitten. She had provided many fond memories and would not soon be forgotten. As for her, she didn't seem to mind, it was as though she knew a new class would soon follow.

"Fort Benning Jump School" class picture taken during the second week of training. The class was comprised of men from the Army as well as members of UDT-11 and UDT-12. Each Team member turned his left shoulder toward the camera so his Team patch would show.

A fully deployed T-10 parachute after static line jump. This is one of the first pictures taken of a Team member jumping from a helicopter during a UDT training exercise.

34. A NIGHT IN NOVEMBER

If you were alive on the twenty-second of November 1963 and older than six, you will remember where you were and what you were doing on that particular day and at the exact time President Kennedy was assassinated. This, more than any other single event, will forever be imbedded in the collective mind of Americans who lived through this tumultuous period in history. I am, however, getting ahead of myself, so in order to keep this story on track, I must take you back to a point in time several months prior to that particular date.

It was the end of September 1963 when Mr. Witter, an officer in Underwater Demolition Team Twelve, and I received orders to pack our gear and report to the Team's overseas headquarters in the Philippines. We were to hitchhike from San Diego to Subic Bay and then join a UDT-12 detachment that had arrived several months earlier. I know, hitchhiking across the Pacific Ocean, to a foreign country, must sound a little strange. After all, it isn't exactly like sticking out your thumb and waiting to see who will pick you up. But, in the Teams, this wasn't an uncommon practice during the early sixties, a time when money was scarce and flights overseas expensive. Therefore, we were ordered to drive to San Francisco and then catch a hop, or military flight, to Hawaii. From there, we were to do our best to find space on any military transport headed to Japan, and then a final flight to Subic Bay.

Mr. Witter was originally from the bay area, so we first drove to his parents' home near San Francisco. Once there, we were able to negotiate space on a military transport that would be leaving for Hawaii in two days. I don't remember the name of Mr. Witter's mother, but his father's name was Dean, and they lived in a beautiful home overlooking the San Francisco Bay. I spent the first night at the Witter home and was totally overwhelmed by the opulence to which they were accustomed. That evening at dinner, I was introduced to the complexities of eating an artichoke, a task that I had never undertaken until that time. Though I was out of my realm, the Witter family proved to be gracious hosts, and I enjoyed my one-night stay with them. The second night, I spent at Travis Air Force Base, just outside of San Francisco. Then, on the third day, our journey began. Our first stop was Hawaii where we spent several days before securing a flight with a detachment of First Force Recon Marines, who were on their way to Japan. I knew a few of these men from parachute jumps that we made together into the Del Mar Racetrack, just north of San Diego. We had kind of an uncomfortable relationship, but that was always the situation when men from the Teams and Marines were put together. This flight, which we shared with the Marines, wouldn't be the last time that we would deal with these men on this detachment. We were scheduled to once again work together, performing beach reconnaissance, off the Coast of Vietnam.

    The flight was uneventful, and we arrived in Japan, where we spent several more days before catching our final hop to Subic Bay in the Philippines, our WESTPAC home. When we arrived, I was excited and looked forward to seeing my fellow teammates and friends who had arrived in Subic Bay several months earlier. I entered the barracks only to find that most of the men were away on a special operation but scheduled to return later that evening. I found my cubicle and started to unpack my gear when I heard a familiar voice coming down the hall. You could never mistake the voice of Gary Lanphier, especially if he had a few beers under his belt. Our UDT detachment shared a barracks with other base personnel, and Gary was giving everyone he met along the way a hard time. That was Gary and from the sound of things, the men he was verbally assaulting had heard it all before.

As he passed my cubicle, Gary looked in, saw me, and started shouting. He ran in and when I reached out my hand to shake his, he hit me square on the jaw. The next thing I knew, I was on my back, and Gary was kneeling over me laughing and shouting about how great it was to see me. He had a smile on his face that said he was happy that I was there but each time he said so, he would again hit me in the face. No telling how long this would have continued if I hadn't been able to break loose by flipping Gary over my head. We struggled to our feet, threw several more punches, and then set down to talk and catch up on all that had happened during the prior two months. While this may sound a little strange to those of you who are not familiar with the way of men in the Teams, in actuality, and especially for Gary, this wasn't an uncommon way to greet someone he liked. I often thought I would be better off if Gary didn't like me; then, the only thing I would have had to do is to stay out of his way.

Apparently Gary had just returned from liberty and his favorite pastime, kicking Marine butt. He had found that by visiting the local Subic Bay bars, frequented by Marines, he would almost certainly be guaranteed a fight. To accomplish this, Gary would simply walk into one of these Marine bars, jump up on a table and challenge anyone in the place. This came to be Gary's favorite pastime and as the saying goes, "The more he fought, the tougher he got." One thing I do know, Gary became one of the toughest men in the Teams and although he didn't win every fight, whenever he did lose, he would always go back to rectify that loss.

My time in Subic Bay passed quickly, and before I knew it, we were well into the month of November. Then came the twenty-second and the events of that unforgettable day in 1963. What happened that day remains as vivid in my mind as the day it happened nearly forty years ago. Actually, it wasn't day at all for those who lived in the Philippines. Due to the time differential, it was night. Early that evening, ten to twelve men from our detachment had crashed a "black shoe" or regular navy party, up on the hill, where sailors permanently stationed in Subic Bay were housed. For those who don't know, the saying "black shoe" is simply a slang expression used to differentiate between men in the regular navy and those in the Teams and is a term frequently used by Team members. Like most parties, this one started out innocently enough but became more and more animated as the evening progressed. Then, by twenty-three hundred hours, or eleven p.m., things were getting totally out of hand. I had been patiently listening to some mouthy black shoe, preaching his philosophy on life, until I finally decided I could take no more and asked him to shut it off. He found my request to be offensive, grabbed my shirt and with as much force as he could muster, ripped it off my back. At that I gave him a solid shot to the stomach and then a right cross to the jaw, and he went down. The party came to a halt, and one of his friends picked up a bottle and moved in behind me to hit me on the back of my head. All of this happened as I knelt over my prey, asking if he wanted to continue expounding his views. Then, before his friend had a chance to put his bottle to good use, one of my teammates picked up another bottle and hit him on the head, which immediately dropped him through his shorts. Everything was happening in slow motion, but unlike it is always portrayed in the old western movies, a full whiskey bottle won't necessarily break when you use it as a weapon. I can still remember being taken back by this fact as I stood there looking at this person who was nonetheless unconscious and down for the count. That thought lasted for no more than several seconds because the real fight was now underway. Though we were outnumbered, it didn't take long before we had gained the upper hand and finished off the last of the black shoes who had unwittingly decided they wanted a piece of the action. Then, just as we were starting to party once more, the Navy Shore Patrol arrived, sirens whaling. When they came through the door, I thought that our fight would be extended, by now adding them to the fracas, but that was not why they had come up the hill. To our surprise, the Shore Patrol announced that President Kennedy had been assassinated and they had been ordered to deliver us to a pier, in Subic Bay, where a submarine, the U.S.S. *Perch*, was now being loaded with our gear.

    Kennedy's assassination had come as a blow to everyone at the party; it was hard for us to believe. We were all stunned by this news, and most of the women were crying. Kennedy had not only been a great President, admired by most Americans, he had also been a sailor who served estimably during World War II. In addition, he had taken great interest in the men assigned to the Underwater Demolition Teams and had recently ordered the formation of the SEAL Teams. He would be sorely missed by a nation who put their trust in this great man.

    As we came down from the hill, there was little to be joyous about and absolutely no conversation between the men who such a short time before were totally raising hell. In addition, we had no idea why we were in such a hurry to get to the waiting submarine. However, we would soon learn that it had to do with the potential escalation of the conflict currently underway in Vietnam. We made a brief stop at our barracks, to pick up our personal belongings, and then boarded the U.S.S. *Perch* not yet knowing what lay ahead.

    It would be hard to adequately explain what it is like to be confined on a World War II Diesel Submarine, for a prolonged period of time, but I will try. The U.S.S. *Perch* was built to accommodate the normal complement of men required to operate the boat and that with very few creature comforts. In addition, this is a very small boat, when compared to the Nuclear Submarines that comprise today's Submarine Navy. Even for the crew, there is not a sufficient number of berths to allow each man to have his own, so while one man is on duty, the man not on duty sleeps. When it is time for the off duty man to go on duty, the man coming off duty takes over the bunk. While these boats were never intended to be comfortable, they were practical and, over the years, had proven to be extremely successful and lethal. There were roughly twenty men from our UDT-12 detachment, in addition to the regular crew of the submarine, scheduled to embark on this operation. So what about twenty extra men who will have to be accommodated in this already confined space? It was decided that the majority of us would be quartered in the aft torpedo compartment. There were no bunks to accommodate us, only the deck and torpedoes that would now serve as our sleeping quarters for the duration of this trip. On numerous occasions, during training and in the Teams, we had operated from submarines but never for an extended period of time and at this time, no one knew exactly how long this deployment would last. Dealing with adversity was a standard mode of operation in the Teams, and we would just have to make the best of this crowded and uncomfortable situation.

If there was one thing that could ease the tensions of operating aboard a submarine, it would have to be the food, and the *Perch* was no exception. I was told that the crew of the *Perch* ate more rice than the crew aboard the average aircraft carrier. At first I thought they were kidding but by the end of this deployment, I had become a believer. Rice was served with every meal, and it was good. So good in fact that I have never been able to find rice that could compare. I don't know what the cooks did, but it was as good with scrambled eggs as it was with a nice juicy steak. In order to feed the men on board, prior to leaving port, provisions were crammed into every conceivable space that did not accommodate electronics equipment or other gear required to run the boat. In addition to these already confined quarters, our detachment had brought aboard diving equipment, small inflatable boats, weapons, and other reconnaissance gear that would be needed at our final destination.

It took several days before we could finally agree on a means to accommodate our twenty-man detachment, but we did find a way. My place was on one of the torpedoes, and that is where I spent most of my time. The aft torpedo compartment was so crowded that you could not move around without inconveniencing several of the other men so most of the time, you just stayed put. This is extremely difficult for men who were accustomed to doing calisthenics, running, and swimming each day. It was our job to stay in excellent condition, and here we were without enough room to even run in place. Then each morning at zero five hundred hours, or five a.m., it would happen. The crew on duty would vent the boat. While this may not sound like much to the average person, you can take my word for it when I say it was a very big thing for our twenty-man UDT Detachment. To vent the boat, the on-duty crew would send a surge of air thru the boat to vent the bad air and replenish it with fresh air. The bad air would be expelled as a bubble out into the ocean and with it came all of the foul air from the several heads aboard the boat. I can in no way describe the horrible stench that came thru the aft torpedo compartment each morning. It would wake each and every one of us out of a sound sleep. There was no way to overcome the smell, and believe me we all tried. Some men slept with their swim mask on, one of the men put a clothespin on his nose, but nothing worked. No matter what you did, the odor permeated and triumphed.

Days turned into a week, then two, and all the while we traveled submerged during the day. This was to be a stealth operation, and the skipper of the *Perch* would only surface at night, when the ship's batteries required recharging, and then only under the cover of darkness and when absolutely necessary. We had entered the South China Sea and though we didn't know it at the time, we were running up and down the coast waiting to pick up three Navy SEAL's who were being shuttled in to meet us for a joint operation.

Late one night, of the third week, we were awakened and told to go up on deck and assist loading the gear of three SEAL Team-One members who had just arrived from Coronado. We had pulled alongside a Navy High Speed Transport, actually a small destroyer that both UDT and SEAL Teams operated from. As the SEAL's were coming aboard, other men from our detachment were ordered to transfer themselves and their gear to the ship that had dropped off the SEALs. I would stay aboard the *Perch*, with four other men, and assist in a reconnaissance operation that involved the SEALs.

It was nice seeing these men and catching up on all that had been happening back home. They tried to explain how a new rock group from Britain, called the Beatles, had broken onto the scene and how their music was sweeping Americans, especially teenage girls, off their feet. We were told they had long hair and that their music was charged and much different from the music we were accustomed to. I couldn't imagine what a singing beetle looked or sounded like and decided I would just have to wait and find out for myself when we returned from this detachment. However, the main topic of conversation centered on the assassination of President Kennedy and how his death had negatively impacted the American people who were still in mourning.

Many things had changed during the two months since I had arrived in Subic Bay. Little did I know how much our world would change over the next few years or just what awaited all of us who lived that day in November, the day President Kennedy was assassinated.

Somewhere on the South China Sea. Boat coxswain (in hat) – Gary Kruger; off his right shoulder – Nick Nickelson; between Gary and Nick – George Layton; arms outstretched – Regie "Bruda" Abrigo.

35. FROM UDT TO SEAL

We had just completed a tour of duty in the Far East and were flying home to Coronado, our primary duty station in the good old Continental United States. During the 1960's, the Far East Headquarters for the Teams was Subic Bay, the Philippines. Subic Bay was centrally located and made for a fast and easy deployment to practically any single location in the Far East, especially Vietnam. From this Subic Bay duty station, men from UDT-12 made the first deployment to Vietnam in 1962. This marked the first time, but by no means the last, that men from both UDT and SEAL Teams would deploy to Vietnam. From that time forward every Far East detachment would spend time in Vietnam conducting beach reconnaissance and covert operations in support of the U.S. military buildup that was taking place at that time.

As our plane touched down at the North Island Naval Air Station there was a new sense of life and excitement exhibited by all aboard the plane. We were energized to finally be back home and on Coronado Island. It had been a long six months and every member of the detachment was anxious to see loved ones and re-connect with his family. Returning from a long deployment or operation was always something to look forward to and this was certainly no exception. A bus was waiting to take the bachelors back to the Amphibious Base while family members waited to take their husbands home for a reunion and well deserved leave.

After we had exited the plane and picked up our gear word came down through the ranks that Dee Van Winkle and I were to report to an airplane hanger not far from where our airplane had taxied to a halt. Nothing more was said except that we were to place our gear on the bus and it would be taken to the Team compound and stowed until we returned. We were ordered to do this on the double and while this all seemed a little bit strange we knew better than to question what we were ordered to do. We hurriedly placed our gear on the bus and quickly found our way to the appointed hanger.

Before I go much further, I should tell you a little about Dee Van Winkle. Dee was a "meat eater" or true Team Operator. He was a remarkable High School athlete and turned down a number of offers to play College football because he wanted to be a frogman. Dee was a fun person to be around and when on liberty, you could always tell where Dee was because there would be a bevy of young women wherever he went. The women loved his boyish good looks and muscular build, plus the fact that he always wore a smile and was never at a loss for words. The only problem for the rest of us; when you went on liberty with Dee you could be assured that you had no chance with the women until Dee decided which one he would spend the evening with. With that now decided, the remaining women were then left to pick from Dee's friends who stood on the sidelines. Dee's most admirable quality was that he was as tough as he was good looking. Whether in a fight or playing sports he was probably the most physical man in the Teams. He was a relentless adversary and a man who would rather die than quit or loose. In a fistfight or combat situation he was the man you would choose to cover your back. Dee could also do something that I would have thought impossible if I didn't see him do it. He could curl his toes under the balls of his feet then raise himself up and walk around on the tops of his toes. I know, you are saying what's the big deal. Well, one night Dee climbed up on a two to three foot high wall and with his toes curled under his feet jumped down on the tops of his curled under toes. He then jumped up and down and ran around on his toes. All I could think was wow if I tried that I would be in casts for months. Anyway, Dee was one hell of a good man and when ordered to report to the hanger, I knew that whatever was in store for us, I was glad that he and I were called to do it together.

Having arrived at the hanger we were surprised to see three men from SEAL Team One waiting there. They told us not to talk or ask questions but to move quickly into the hanger where we would be briefed for a simple mission. We did as we were told and when we entered the hanger found a portable blackboard partially covered with a cloth, resting on an easel. Near the easel was a table with a map, compass, paper and pencils. Next to the table were several other items that included two web belts with canteens, flairs, and k-bar knives. In addition, there were two medical packs, two main and reserve parachutes, two football helmets, and two foul weather jackets.

We were then told to retrieve the pencils and paper, stand in front of the blackboard, and pay close attention to the briefing that would be given by one of the SEAL Team members. From the briefing we learned we would be flown to a mountainous area southeast of San Diego near Otay Reservoir. This is an area that both UDT and SEAL Teams use as a drop zone for training and parachute jumps so Dee and I were familiar with the area. We were then given map coordinates and told that at a specific location, marked on a map, we were to retrieve an American flag that had been sealed in a can then buried. The area that would serve as our drop zone was relatively flat and very near the mountains where the flag was buried. We would be given four hours to find the flag and return to the drop zone for extraction, a relatively short time frame. We were then taken to the table and shown a map and the location of the buried flag.

The briefing now ended we were then told that we could not ask questions about this operation nor would we be told why we were chosen. However, if we were successful and completed the assignment, within the prescribed time frame, we would be told everything we needed to know and all our questions would be answered. On the other hand, if we did not succeed then we would be told nothing and returned to the Team Compound as if none of this had ever happened. We were then ordered to fold up and stow the map and compass and pick up our foul weather jackets and parachutes and follow the men from SEAL Team One to a waiting helicopter. When I asked if we would be given a radio we were told that a radio wouldn't be necessary because there would be someone nearby at all times observing our progress.

Dee and I looked at each other, packed up our provisions, then picked up our parachutes and foul weather jackets and headed for the door. We were still wearing our khaki uniforms and jump boots so we were basically ready to undertake an operation we didn't understand, couldn't ask questions about, and one which at that time made absolutely no sense. The timing of this operation was probably the most confusing factor being that it had been scheduled immediately upon our return from a six-month detachment to the Far East.

As we walked from the hanger, two of the SEALs walked to a waiting truck and the third told us to follow him to a helicopter that was already warmed up and ready to go. In the Teams we often jumped from helicopters especially if the Drop Zone (DZ) was relatively near by. We climbed aboard and were soon underway for a short twenty to twenty-five mile flight to Lake Otay and Otay Mountain. Dee and I had yet to talk to each other about what was happening but that could wait until after the jump and we were on the ground.

It was great being home again and as we lifted off and flew southeast across the bay it only reinforced the fact that I loved Coronado, San Diego, and this southern most county in California. I always looked forward to Team deployments but it couldn't compare to the feeling of arriving back in Coronado at the conclusion of that deployment. And while it would have been nice to spend a little time in Coronado, before being sent on another operation, I think both Dee and I were anxious to find out why we had been chosen for this mission. As we gained altitude we geared up and took up our positions on the floor and in the open door of the helicopter with our feet extended out and resting on one of the skids. Then, as we drew nearer to the DZ the chopper started making broad circles while climbing ever higher. We knew we were there when the jumpmaster threw a streamer out the door and we watched as it fell toward earth. One final adjustment by the pilot then we were tapped on the shoulder and we jumped.

On the ground we folded up our parachutes took out the map and compass, oriented ourselves, took bearings and started toward the mountain which stood approximately a mile from where we had landed. We left the parachutes and started to jog in line with the coordinates that had been laid out for us on the map. We would be required to cross several small hills then climb to an elevation of approximately thirty-five hundred feet in order to reach our destination. Within one and one-half hours we were in the general vicinity of the buried flag but now the hard part, searching the area by using a search pattern that would prevent us from wasting time and therefore missing the target and having to do it over again. The pattern that we established worked and along with a little luck it took us roughly one hour to find the buried can and to retrieve the flag. We now had two hours until pick up so we were able to take our time returning to the DZ. On the way back we tried to speculate about why we had been assigned this operation and came to the conclusion that we were being considered for a transfer to SEAL Team One. We would later find out that our assumptions were correct but for now we had to keep hustling back to the DZ and the pre-appointed extraction area.

We reached the DZ with roughly thirty minutes to spare and now did a better job of folding our parachutes. We then sat down to wait. We hadn't been waiting long when a Team truck approached with three men from SEAL Team One. When we turned over the flag they congratulated us and said we had been given this mission as a test. By successfully completing the test we were going to be given the opportunity of a lifetime and that would be to transfer from UDT to SEAL. If we accepted this offer we would be taken back to the Team Compound and would then start the paperwork. It was a great opportunity but Dee almost immediately declined. He stated that he appreciated the offer but wanted to continue to operate, as a member of UDT-12. He further stated that he wasn't interested in going to all of the schools that the men assigned to SEAL Team One were required to attend. As for me, I also declined but for a different reason. In order to accept it would be necessary for me to extend my enlistment for two more years and I wasn't certain that I wanted to do that at this time. Surprisingly there were no questions asked and we were told to climb into the back of the truck. We then returned to the Team Compound and UDT-12.

I was later given another opportunity to transfer into SEAL Team One but that happened very near the end of my enlistment. Again, I declined. At this point I had decided to leave the service and take a job in the private sector. My wife was pregnant with our son Kenny and it just seemed like the right thing to do. I will admit that there have been times when I questioned my decision to leave the Teams and if I had it to do over again I don't know if I would make the same decision. I look at the Teams today and all they have to offer and wish that I could start it all over again. I still see Dee at reunions but don't know how he feels. It really doesn't make any difference what we think now because no matter what, we can look back and know that we were a part of the Teams when everything we did was new and exciting. We were a part of the Teams during a special time when things were just starting to change. In retrospect, who could ask for more?

36. THE STANDING FISHERMAN

Like everything we do in life, if a task is done repeatedly it soon becomes just a part of the routine and after a prolonged period of time it is completed without even giving it a second thought. That was the way it was for men in the Teams, assigned to the otherwise gruesome task of body search and recovery. During BUDS Training we learned well the intricacies of body search and recovery and we would carry this particular type of training into the Teams where, only too often, it would be put to practical use.

While everyone was required to perform this task, and it was done without hesitation, there were several men who really had a tough time doing what was considered part of every day life by most. Tom MacDonald just happened to be one of the men who didn't care to deal with or, for that matter, discuss issues pertaining to the dead. Tom didn't much care how a person died; as far as he was concerned he would just as soon leave it alone or let others deal with the particulars. I am not certain but I think his feelings about death and dying stem for a negative childhood experience, one that changed his outlook on this subject forever.

Regardless of the fact that Tom didn't like to be involved in body search and recovery, if he was on duty when the call came in, he was required to join the search party whether he liked it or not. But believe me when I say this, when Tom was required to join in body search and recovery, he never went softly into the night. No indeed, Tom did everything imaginable to exclude himself from this assignment. However, in the Teams, when your number is called you will accept the duties and responsibilities of the assignment no matter what your personal feelings happen to be. Therefore, when required to join in this macabre task, though kicking and screaming, Tom would reluctantly do what was required of him.

As was mentioned earlier, for most men in the Teams, this became a routine task and, in time, body recovery had little or no impact on them. For those men who found a body, during a recovery operation, it was a simple matter of swimming the body to the recovery boat then returning to the Team compound and getting back into the daily routine. Besides, the normal complement of men, required to conduct a body search and recovery, consisted of no less than ten men. Taking this into account, the chances that you and your swim buddy would actually find the body was limited by shear numbers to twenty percent. Not that percentages were important, or I should say that percentages were not important to most of the men doing the body search, for Tom percentages meant everything.

Sadly for Tom, percentages never seemed to work in his favor. Quite the contrary, it seems that every body search Tom was ever assigned to, he and his swim partner found the body. As much as he hated this job, Tom was a "dead body" magnet. It got to be a laughing matter among the men in the Teams. If Tom were to be involved in a body search and recovery operation the standing joke became; just put Tom in the water, the body will find its way to him and the rest of us don't even have to get wet. I am not trying to be disrespectful to the dead; I am just trying to relate what seemed apparent to everyone who accompanied Tom on one of these exercises. It seemed to us that the reason Tom was so successful in this enterprise stemmed from the fact that he hated doing it so much. I don't know if there is some universal law involved in situations like this but in Tom's case, there was some unknown reason why he always turned up with the victim.

To aggravate an already difficult assignment, or at least as far as Tom was concerned, were those occasions when he was required to conduct a body search at night. For example, late one night Tom found the victim when we were conducting a body search in the Panama Cannel Zone. While Tom's swim partner stayed with the body, Tom shot to the surface like a rocket. He was moving so fast when he reached the surface that his body landed inside the Inflatable Boat Small (IBS). A Herculaneum accomplishment given the fact that Tom was wearing a twin-ninety aqualung, a weight belt, and other assorted diving gear. All in all, this equipment would have weighed in the neighborhood of ninety to one hundred pounds. In addition, swimming to the surface as fast as he did, Tom was lucky not to have suffered a severe case of the bends. The only harm done this evening was to Tom's honor. He eventually did calm down but swore this would be his last body recovery, no matter what.

Well, as you might have guessed, this did not bring to an end Tom's days of body search and recovery. No indeed, Tom was once again called upon to join a group of men selected to search for a fisherman who had fallen overboard, went straight to the bottom, and was never seen again. This drowning happened on a wide, deep, and slow moving river; therefore, the search and recovery would prove a challenge because it was unlike diving for a body in a lake or the ocean. Normally, in a case like this, the body moves down river with the current. It then becomes the job of a rescue team to stretch a net across the river, approximately one-half to one mile from where the man had fallen overboard, and wait for the body to come to them. Not this time however, it had been two days and the body had yet to be recovered. In an effort to expedite the search, a call was placed to Team Headquarters and men were gathered to conduct the search.

After arriving at the scene and having received a briefing by the sheriffs department it was decided that the only way to conduct this search would be by moving upstream and stretching a rope across the river. Twenty swimmers, wearing aqualungs, would then enter the water and take up positions; two arm lengths separating each swimmer. When all swimmers were in place and the signal given, the line of men would sink to the bottom and while holding onto the rope and the hand of the swimmer to either side, simply let the current gently move the swimmers down stream until contact was made with the victim. This seemed to be a simple and easy solution to the problem.

Have you forgotten that Tom MacDonald was a part of this recovery exercise? Well he was and the real excitement was yet to come. Like similar exercises, Tom had done everything imaginable to exclude himself from this operation. But as hard as Tom tried the more convinced the Chief in charge of the dive was that Tom would be a member of the swim line. Tom's pleads to be a part of the shore party, or a member of the boat crew drew little consideration; in fact, all this bargaining did was reinforce the fact that Tom would be involved as a diver. While everyone got a good laugh out of all that Tom was doing, to Tom this was a very serious matter. The final outcome, Tom was now in line with the other men and in deep water.

It didn't take long before the line of swimmers passed the area where the fisherman had fallen overboard. Then it happened, as had been the case on other body searches Tom was the first to come in contact with the body. This particular recovery would prove to be different from other recoveries, not only for Tom, but also for everyone assigned to this operation. The fisherman wasn't lying on the bottom of the river as everyone had expected; this man was standing fully upright like he was ready to take a Sunday stroll. The man had been wearing waist high fishing boots when he fell overboard and as he sank to the bottom they filled with water. His decent ended when his feet hit the bottom and apparently that is the way he had remained until the very moment Tom's head came in contact with the fishing boots, at about ankle level. When Tom looked up and saw the man standing there with his head down and looking directly at him, body waving back and forth in the slow moving current, he almost had a heart attack. Tom screamed out, then let go of the hands of the men on either side of him and like a bolt of lightening took off for the surface. Like he had done in Panama, when Tom broke the surface he cleared the side of the Inflatable Boat Small (IBS), tied alongside the recovery boat, and nearly crushed the two-man boat crew who had no idea what had caused this to happen. Unlike the Panama operation, Tom was speechless. Yes, he had been so frightened by this experience that he couldn't say a word for about five minutes. Then, when he finally recovered, Tom repeated over and over that this was the last time and that he would die before ever being involved in another body search and recovery.

  As shaken as Tom had been by this experience, he wasn't alone. The sight of that man standing there, looking down at the men who had come to recover him, unnerved several others. Something happened that day and it was totally unexpected. It was something the men had not been prepared for and while it seemed to surprise everyone, it had a much greater impact on Tom. Time would pass and this event would be forgotten by most but I doubt that was the case with Tom. And for those who wonder if Tom was ever involved in another body recovery, I can't answer that question. But like other men in the Teams, ordered to conduct an operation that they would have rather not been called upon to support, if given the assignment Tom would have done what he was ordered to do, he was an operator.

37. A TIME OF REFELCTION

At the time, it seemed like nothing more than an average couple of days spent as a member of UDT-12. Now, nearly forty years later, as I reflect back on the events of that operation, I know it was anything but average. To hear the words Underwater Demolition Teams still makes me feel good. Like most veterans, I am very proud of the time I spent in the service but, even more than most, because my time in the Service was spent with an elite special-forces unit known today as Navy SEAL Teams.

The couple of days I refer to happened during an operation that would qualify UDT-12 as combat ready, for a two-year period, and is highly important in the eyes of top Navy brass. This Operation Readiness Review (ORR) involves not only UDT but also Navy ships carrying supplies as well as Marines. The Marines conduct beach landings after UDT has performed reconnaissance of all landing beaches, the inland area surrounding those beaches, and cleared any obstacles that may have been placed to prevent the Marines from coming ashore. It would be the job of six swim teams, comprised of two men each, to conduct initial beach and inland reconnaissance of six separate beaches and report back to Command Operations so a landing beach could be identified. At that point, other UDT swimmers would be dispatched to locate and destroy any obstacles and clear the way for the Marines.

Along with members of the six swim teams, I boarded the submarine, U.S.S. *Perch*, and headed for a pre-determined drop location four miles offshore from the designated beaches we were to reconnoiter. The *Perch* was one of the few remaining World War II diesel submarines still in commission and was primarily used by UDT/SEAL Teams for training and/or special operations. For two days prior to the start of the ORR, we ran submerged to avoid detection. Then at twenty-two hundred hours, or ten at night, we started our lockout procedure in preparation for a four-mile swim to our designated beaches.

The principal purpose of the lockout chamber is to provide a mechanism for the submarine's crew to escape to the surface in case of an emergency underwater. The chamber is cylindrical in shape with three hatches: one on top, one on the side, one on the bottom, and can easily accommodate two swimmers at one time. The swimmers enter the chamber thru the bottom hatch, close and flood the chamber, turn the flood valve off when the water level reaches the top of the side hatch, then open the side hatch, and swim up a line (rope) tied to the periscope. A second line is attached to the periscope with twelve spaced knots, one for each swimmer. As each swimmer reaches the surface, he then takes his place in line, holding onto one of the knots, while waiting for the remainder of the swimmers to complete their lockout procedure. During this lockout period, the submarine is traveling at roughly one to two knots, or just above stall speed. This enables the six swim teams to remain together until the submarine's skipper dips the periscope three times, the predetermined signal for the swimmers to drop off. With that completed, it was then time to make preparations for the four-mile swim to shore.

The night was particularly cold and dark. It was indeed perfect weather for this type of an operation. A storm had brought both wind and rain and that would mean that anyone patrolling the beaches would be cold and not as attentive to their duties as they otherwise might be. Each swimmer wore a wet-suit top and wet-suit bottoms, cutoff just above the knee to prevent chafing. A K-bar knife, mask, UDT fins, life vest, and plastic slate (to write down pertinent data found during the reconnaissance), comprised the basic gear. Each swimmer wore coral shoes and carried a camouflage shirt and pants to wear the following day. There would be no food, but that wouldn't present a problem because if all went well, we would be back aboard the *Perch* the following night at twenty hundred hours or eight p.m.

It would be important to orient ourselves prior to starting the swim to shore because we were to rendezvous with the submarine at roughly the same location the following evening. The trick to getting proper bearings is to line-up two permanent and recognizable lights on shore, place one behind the other, and keep them properly aligned during the entire swim to the beach. By doing this, you would then have a reference the following evening when swimming back to the submarine. This is extremely important if you want to be picked up by the submarine. Missing your pick-up location would mean another swim back to the beach and possibly jeopardizing the entire operation. A four-mile swim takes approximately two hours, so leaving the beach at eighteen hundred hours, six p.m., would put us back at the submarine right on time. The swim to the beach did in fact take two hours, so it was agreed that we would rendezvous at the same location, as we had landed, and depart at eighteen hundred hours the following evening.

At that point, my swim buddy and I headed to a spot just off the open beach and changed into our camouflage shirt and pants. They were wet and did little to keep out the cold. This would be an evening not soon forgotten. The wind howled and blew the rain so hard it felt like pin pricks to the exposed skin. It remained like this for the next six hours.

Now, everyone has experienced being cold and can tell you a story about their coldest moment. But, to someone in the Teams, cold is when your testicles retract back into your stomach. When that happens, you can't move until you reach in with a finger and pull them back out. If you don't, you experience excruciating pain each time you move and, to top it off, you are so cold and uncomfortable that it becomes impossible to gather your bearings and concentrate on the job that lies ahead. In the Teams and during training, you experience this condition often enough that you learn to live with it. It is just part of the job. The hours crept by slowly as Charlie and I lay there in the mud, shivering and doing what little we could to fend off the cold.

I should tell you about Charlie before we go much further. His real name is Hal Tune, but we gave him the nickname Charlie Tuna, yes, because he could swim like a fish. I liked to operate with Charlie because he always gave one hundred percent and never complained no matter how difficult the situation. I was a runner and Charlie a swimmer so we complemented each other and made a good team. One thing I should make clear is that every man in the Teams shared one common trait; each was an operator; otherwise, he wouldn't be in the Teams. This was a special fraternity of brothers and between these men, bonds were forged that can never be broken.

By dawn, the skies had started to clear, and I must admit the prospects of a warm sun gave us both something to look forward to and a reason to be happy. Our night had been spent huddled in a washed-out ravine, several hundred yards off of the beach, so it was important for us to move away from the beach and into the hinterland where shrubs and overgrowth could provide some coverage.

On the beach and the surrounding area were marines, acting as the opposing enemy forces, whose job it was to repel this operation and find us at all cost. We moved slowly thru the brush and then thru a drainage ditch under a freeway that ran parallel to the beach we were to reconnoiter. We then moved to the high ground and took up a position to view the beach and surrounding area. It wasn't until ten hundred hours, or ten a.m., that the warmth of the sun wore thru the cold of the previous night making it possible for us to confront the job that we had been inserted to do. By mid afternoon, we had performed a reconnaissance of our assigned area and settled in until it was time to return to the staging area and the swim back to the submarine.

During the latter part of the afternoon, we had a run-in with a marine patrol but were able to elude them. We then moved out to the area where we had buried our swim gear earlier that morning. I should say where Charlie had buried his swim gear, while I had camouflaged mine near a tree. The spot we had chosen to hide our gear was the same spot the Marines later chose, for a dumpsite, to dispose of empty sea-ration cans and all their trash. It turned out that this decision led to the Marines finding my swim gear but not Charlie's. For me, that was bad news. In the Teams, there is a saying, "In UDT you must learn from the mistakes of others because you won't live long enough to make them all yourself." This was a big mistake and learning experience. For me, it would mean that a very important decision was looming on the horizon.

We made our way back to the staging area, and by eighteen hundred hours, all six-swim teams had reported in. Their missions successfully completed, all were now geared-up and ready to start the two-hour swim back to the submarine. But now a decision had to be made, due to the fact I had no swim gear. I could either make the two-hour swim, without the protection of a wet suit, or surrender to the opposing forces. Now, for those of you who have braved the Pacific Ocean in mid November, I think you might agree that the wise decision would have been to turn myself in. I would have then spent the next three to four days as a prisoner, but after all, this wasn't a real wartime situation. The worst thing that I would have to face was the disgrace of putting myself into this situation to begin with. Without giving it much thought, I chose option one and the swim. This would later turn out to be a near fatal decision, though I didn't know it at the time. To make the swim more bearable for me, Charlie, who I mentioned was a strong swimmer, gave me his swim fins and wet-suit bottoms. Jim Foley, from one of the other swim teams and also a strong swimmer, gave me his life vest and a thicker, reversible t-shirt, known in the Teams as a "blue and gold." With that we started our two-hour swim to the waiting arms of the U.S.S. *Perch*.

    The night was cold, and the weather had started to turn bad once again as a light rain began to fall. The surf was up, and we could see that the ocean was choppy as we made our way into the water. The initial impact of the cold water, as I slipped under a wave, caused me to bite my tongue. It's always a shock to the system when your upper torso and cold water first make contact. With the initial shock behind me, I joined the other swimmers, and we swam out about five or six hundred yards. At this point, we reoriented ourselves by lining-up the two permanent lights we had used to guide us the night before. With that accomplished, we reestablished and set our bearings and then started what would turn out to be the most difficult part of the mission.

    The first hour of the swim was uncomfortable but bearable. The previous night's swim, cold night spent in the mud and rain, and then gathering reconnaissance data during the day had exacted a toll on all twelve men, although none complained. After all, if everything went according to plan, we would be back on board the U.S.S. *Perch* in about an hour. The second hour was more difficult for me. The cold water was starting to take its toll, but I knew that soon this operation would be concluded, so I ignored the pain. In the Teams, you learn to live with pain, and I know some who live by the axiom, "If it doesn't hurt, you aren't trying hard enough." By twenty hundred hours, we had made it to what we felt was our predetermined rendezvous point. The two lights on the beach were still in alignment, and we had been swimming for two hours. Now it was a simple matter of waiting for the submarine to locate us.

President Kennedy had a wooden plaque on his desk with the inscription, "Oh God, thy sea is so great and my boat is so small." I was soon to realize just how small and insignificant twelve men are, floating in the Pacific Ocean, in the dark of night, but in our case, without a boat. Two hours turned into three and by now hypothermia had started taking control. I no longer felt the cold and started slipping in and out of consciousness. I would have visions of things past and things yet to come but during all of this, I cannot remember feeling fear. I could function at some level, but I remember Charlie, or one of the other Team members, pulling the toggle to inflate my life jacket so I wouldn't slip under.

By twenty-two hundred hours, or ten p.m., we had been in the water four hours and were concerned that we would soon have to make the decision to swim back to the beach. Each swimmer carried a flare, one end for night and the other end for day, so we started setting off flares, each at five-minute intervals. After the night flares had been exhausted and the submarine had yet to find us, we started setting off the smoke, or day end of the flare and shining a flashlight on the smoke. We hoped this would alert the submarine to our location, although this seemed like a real long shot. I remember being told that it had been decided that we would return to the beach when I heard loud shouting and saw the submarine slowly approaching. It was twenty-three hundred hours.

The submarine had surfaced to pick us up, and I remember being pulled onto the deck but nothing after that. Two hours later when I regained consciousness, I found myself in the engine room, the warmest place on the boat, snuggling up to one of the diesel engines. The other swim teams and Charlie had reported all details garnered from the reconnaissance, which was then forwarded to Command Operations. Our mission now complete, we remained aboard the submarine and returned to our homeport, Coronado, California.

In a debriefing, our Commanding Officer, Captain Robinson, gave rave reviews to the six swim teams for both the pertinent reconnaissance data gathered and for an unwavering commitment to duty. There wasn't a man who hadn't been pushed to his limit by this operation, but there wasn't a man to ever complain of that night or what might have happened if the swim back to the beach would have been required. Five hours in the frigid waters of the Pacific Ocean on a stormy November night seems like a noble feat and one worthy of praise. But I feel that way now because I am nearly sixty years old and realize that this is a situation not many have faced, or at least faced and lived to tell about. As for the time that it happened, like thousands of related but unrecorded accomplishments that could and should be attributed to members of the Underwater Demolition/SEAL Teams, it will remain just an average couple of days spent in the Teams. And do you know what? That is really all that it was. Oh yes, UDT-12 was awarded the score of Excellent "E" for their overall performance in the Operation Readiness Review.

Nick Nickelson, in full swim gear, standing in front Team training compound.

38. BODY SEARCH AND RECOVERY

As a member of Underwater Demolition Team-12 (UDT-12), I was blessed with many and varied duty assignments. All were exciting and challenging, and some pushed me past previous limits. This was the beauty of being in the Teams; there was seldom a dull moment while there was always a new experience awaiting you each day.

In the Teams, the one assignment least talked about is that of body search and recovery. During training we were taught the various techniques and were prepared to treat this as a normal part of the job. Then, after training it didn't take long before we were required to put this training to practical use. It seemed that there was always a plane or helicopter going down, a grown-up or child drowning, a boating accident, suicide, car going off a bridge, and the list goes on and on. Before long, body search and recovery became a routine task in my daily life, as it was for every other man in the Teams.

Prior to entering the service, I had been a member of a club called the "Colorado Gypsy Divers." Our primary function was that of body recovery. We were trained to respond to emergency calls related to drowning in lakes and rivers, during the summer as well as under the ice in the winter. I was young and found what we did very exciting.

Upon completion of Basic Underwater Demolition SEAL Training (BUDS), I returned home to Colorado on leave. The night after I arrived, I received a call, asking me to assist in a body recovery. Apparently, there had been a young man swimming in a lake, adjacent to a resort hotel in Colorado Springs, who had drowned. I agreed and arrived at approximately twenty-two hundred or ten that night. It was very dark, so the police had set up lights, but no one had entered the water. I could see the friends of the young man who had drowned, sitting on the opposite side of the lake and could sense their anguish. I didn't pay them much more attention as I put on diving gear that the club provided. There were two other members of the Gypsy Divers who had already suited-up and would assist in the recovery. Neither had been involved in a body recovery before that night so I would be the lead diver.

It is always a little eerie diving for a body at night and I could tell that the other two divers were somewhat apprehensive. I instructed them to each take my outstretched hand and to swim on either side of me, as close to the bottom of the lake as possible. We would swim back and forth across the lake until we found the body. We then started the search near where the young man was last seen. The lake was no deeper than twenty-five feet, and the distance from one side to the other was less than two hundred yards. Underwater, it was pitch black, and I couldn't see either of the two divers at my sides. That wasn't a problem, as long as we maintained contact by holding hands. On the second pass, my head came in contact with the body. At that moment, the other two divers realized what had happened, simultaneously squeezed my hand as hard as they could, and headed for the surface. Because this was their first body recovery, I understood what they must have felt. However, the last thing I wanted was to lose the body and have to start the search all over. I was able to break their grasp and grab the body before I lost contact, and then I started to make my way to the surface. I was holding the body from behind, my arms clasped around his chest, as the boat made its way toward us. By this time the other two divers were on the beach, still a little shaken by the whole experience. The boat arrived and as the men in the boat started to pull the young man on board, he was turned around and for the first time, I could see his face. That sight sent a shock thru me that I can feel to this day. It turned out to be a young man I had gone to school with; in fact, his sister and I had graduated from high school two years earlier. I then realized that his friends, those who I had seen sitting on the beach, were also young men I knew from high school. It was a sad night for all involved.

In the future, I would be required to dive for friends that had been lost in the ocean. It was never easy going on a body search for someone you are close to. The thing that was different about the body recovery in Colorado, versus those that would follow, was the fact that I had no idea that I knew the person, until I saw his face when he was pulled into the boat.

On another occasion, I was called upon to join other Team members to locate a helicopter that had crashed into the ocean, several miles off the Silver Strand, south of Coronado. From different onshore military facilities, the Navy was able to triangulate a fix on the helicopter before it crashed into the water. In all appearances, this would be an easy recovery. We arrived at the crash site early in the morning and started the dive. There was no chance that anyone from the four-man crew could have survived so that wasn't a point of concern. We were there to recover the bodies for their families. We were also there to attach a signal locater so the Navy Salvage Divers could retrieve the helicopter. The water was no deeper than fifty feet and with hand-held sonar units, to locate the target; it looked like we would be in and out in no time.

On our initial dive, we found the water to be cloudy and visibility limited. In addition, there were large rocks protruding from the bottom, causing false readings from our hand-held sonar units. Some of the rocks were the size of the helicopter, so the sonar was of little use to us. We spent the entire day diving and groping in the poor visibility and found nothing. We returned to Coronado that night but would be back the next day to complete the mission. However, the second day turned out to be no different than the first, and again we returned home empty handed. We left the area undaunted, knowing we would do better the following day.

Day three turned out to be our lucky day. We had been in the water for no more than thirty minutes when we located the downed helicopter. At this point, the four-man crew had been underwater for five days, and their bodies were starting to decompose. This smell attracts lobsters and fish, and by now they had started to feed on the decaying flesh. For us, this didn't create a problem; in fact, we came prepared for just such an occasion.

When on a body search, if the body had been in the ocean for several days, we always carried burlap sacks. When we located the body, we would first gather the lobsters that were feeding on the body and then place them in the sacks. With that complete, we would then remove what was left of the body, or in this case, bodies. We bagged probably twenty lobsters at this particular site and the remains of the four men. With the men now in body bags, we radioed ahead for a medical team to meet us at a predetermined beach location. We then called our Team office and arranged for other members of Team-12 to meet us as well. They would bring with them one-half of a fifty-gallon drum, wood for a fire and a keg of beer.

The medical unit met us as planned and removed the bodies. Other Team-12 members had also arrived by this time and had the fire going and water boiling. The one-half, fifty-gallon drum was a perfect cauldron. The keg of beer had been tapped, and the only thing missing were the lobsters we brought with us. We threw the lobsters into the boiling water and in no time sat down to the perfect meal of lobster and beer.

The real purpose of this story is to show how indifferently you can treat such matters when you are constantly placed in this type of situation. Death is just an extension of life and something that has to be dealt with. So it was for men in the Teams. While I no longer have to do the things I was required to do in the Teams, I look back upon that part of my life as a learning experience and something that helped me to grow and understand life and death a little better.

    This isn't the first time I have told this story, and it has been my experience that people were often times put off by what we did; they found it offensive. I try to explain that there was nothing we could do for the men that had died, but as for the lobsters, well that was a different matter. We enjoyed the lobster and would do so, under similar circumstances, many times before I left the Teams. I hope when you read this that you can acknowledge the fact that lobsters are scavengers that eat dead things, fish, human, and whatever. If you eat lobster and didn't know this fact, I hope it doesn't put you off your next lobster dinner.

39. RIPTIDE

One phenomenon that we often encounter in the ocean is commonly known as "Riptide." If not treated with respect, a riptide is quite capable of killing, and does far too often, especially young children and adults who do not swim well or are not in good physical condition. When I say respect, I mean just that, but not fear. Riptides or rips are a common occurrence on the West Coast and take lives only because far too many people who enter the ocean simply don't understand how to deal with them.

As a member of Underwater Demolition Team-12 (UDT-12), I can recall several instances where we were called upon to locate a person who had drowned in the ocean not far from the beach. If the person had been missing for only a short time, the first thing we did was look for a riptide. You can usually spot a rip, because it appears as though the water it controls is going out to sea from near the beach. While the water on either side of the rip is breaking on shore, the water in the rip is going in the opposite direction. A rip will also change the way waves break near the beach, because the area it encompasses is usually flat.

Of critical importance is what you know and do if ever caught in a riptide. This is a situation that can be easily remedied if you don't panic. Panic is the key reason most people die in a riptide related drowning. So there will be no misunderstanding, if ever pulled into a riptide, just observe the following. You will know you are in a rip if you find yourself farther from shore than you had imagined, and as you try to swim back to the beach, you actually get nowhere, but just keep going farther out to sea. At this point, simply stop swimming and let the rip take you until you see that you are no longer in its grasp. A riptide loses its power as it gets into deeper water farther from the beach. So, if you let the rip take you until it loses its control, you can simply swim to the right or left of the rip and then swim back to the beach.

Most people drown because the first thing they do is exert all of their energy swimming in the rip, back toward the beach. If you do this, I can assure you that it won't work; you will simply tire yourself out. Swimming against a riptide is like swimming up stream, against a strong current. A riptide controls a very narrow ban of water and generally only goes out to sea one to two hundred yards. Another thing you can do, when you realize you are in a riptide, is swim to one side or the other, horizontal to the beach, until you are free from the pull of the rip. At this point, you simply swim to shore. The main thing you must remember is "Do not panic!" Just sit back and enjoy the ride; it's as simple as that.

As I mentioned earlier, when we were called on to recover a body and found that the person had been caught in a rip, there was one thing we did first. We would swim into the riptide and let it carry us until it ran out and was no longer pulling us to sea. At that point, we would swim down and start the body search. Not in every case, but in most, the body would be right there. Sadly, those searches could have been prevented had those people known and applied a few simple tactics when dealing with a riptide.

40. LEO HAMEL - MASTER CHIEF

I first met Leo Hamel on the grinder, behind the Team Compound, when I graduated from BUDS. Leo was much older than the average young frogman who made up the ranks of the Teams, during the early 60's, but he was nonetheless a warrior. Leo had served during the Korean War and had been promoted through the ranks to the highest level an enlisted man can attain in the Navy, that of Master Chief. Leo loved the Navy, his family, lifting weights, and working out, and I would bet in that order. And, because lifting weights was also one of my passions, Leo and I hit it off immediately.

They called the area where we worked out "the grinder" because this was the area where we did calisthenics or Physical Training (P.T.) each morning after muster. It was also the area where we would go to lift weights, play handball or volleyball, and where any number of classes in marshal arts was taught. This was the area where we went each morning and, rain or shine, "ground it out" to stay in peak physical condition. Therefore, this area became appropriately known to one and all as simply "the grinder".

Leo was not quite six feet tall but he was huge, especially in the areas of chest and arms. He loved to do bench presses and could easily handle 350 lbs. in multiple repetitions. While this may have been admirable, the one thing I respected most about Leo was the fact that he didn't swear, drink, or smoke and as far as I knew, he never did. In the Teams it was rare indeed to find an individual who didn't over indulge in at least one of these three vices.

Leo's primary rate was that of Ship Fitter and this then carried over into the career he planned to pursue upon his retirement from the Navy. Several years prior to his retirement Leo received permission from the Navy and started a small plumbing and refrigeration business. On occasion he would do small jobs for Team members and businesses in and around San Diego and Coronado. Of course, he would only do this when he wasn't on duty; Leo would do nothing that might be construed as a conflict of interest or interfere with the life he had chosen and his love of the Navy. It is important to understand one thing, the men in the Teams, during the 60's, weren't paid the big bucks. Even though they received double hazardous duty pay for diving, demolitions, and parachuting, their yearly salary was diminutive to say the least. I know that I just mentioned three hazardous duty areas, so didn't I mean triple hazardous duty pay? No, a man in the Teams could only receive hazardous duty pay for two of the three hazardous duty disciplines for which he was qualified; that was the way of the military. By the way, double hazardous pay amounted to an extra $120 a month or $60 for each of the two disciplines a man remained up to date and qualified in.

One Saturday afternoon Leo received a call from the owner of a bar that just happened to be a local Team hangout in Coronado. It seems that the refrigeration system had crashed and it was critical that it be brought back on line before all of the beer became undrinkable. When Leo arrived he was greeted not only by the owner of the establishment but also by several Teammates who had been assisting the owner, by drinking as much beer as they could consume in hopes this would help alleviate the problem.

The afternoon was unusually hot so not only was the refrigeration system, required to cool the beer, on the fritz; also, the refrigeration system used to cool the bar was down for the count. Leo assessed the situation and went immediately to work. Due to the heat and close working conditions it wasn't long before Leo was sweating profusely. On several occasions the owner asked Leo if he would care for a beer but Leo politely refused and only drank water. As the afternoon wore on Leo's Teammates, who by now were feeling no pain, started to chide Leo for drinking nothing stronger than water and asking if he would like a nice cold beer or something other than the usual dull water. Leo politely refused and went about his work, paying them little attention.

Now everyone in the Teams knew Chief Hamel didn't drink so if one of his Teammates could convince him to do otherwise it would be considered a major coup. Therefore, they continued to work on him but to no avail. It may sound a little strange, and it undoubtedly is, but this is the way of men in the Teams. Mind games, it was simply a matter of playing mind games. Then R.E., one of Leo's Teammates, came up with a plan. He told Leo that he should stop with the water and drink orange juice or something that would put spent vitamins back into his system, a drink that would replenish lost energy. Leo saw through this one knowing that R.E. would probably add Vodka, as he surely would have done. Then R.E. suggested a drink made from fresh strawberries and crushed ice. R.E. went on to tell Leo that it was simply a "smoothie" that would not only cool him off but would provide a boost from the strawberries as well. The clincher came when R.E. told Leo that he could watch the bartender make the drink. This was a sure sign that R.E. only had Leo's best interest at heart. With that, Leo agreed and watched intently as the strawberries and ice were placed in the blender and crushed to a silky smoothness. "This is wonderful" Leo exclaimed, as he drank the heavenly concoction with gusto, thanked the bartender and R.E., and then went back to work.

It wasn't long before Leo asked for another of his new favorite drinks and R.E. eagerly agreed; however, this time a new ingredient would be added. Unlike R.E., Leo wasn't familiar with strawberry daiquiris and the fact that you really couldn't taste the alcohol once it was added and therefore wouldn't know it was even in the drink until you had had several and by then it would be too late. R.E. instructed the bartender to add a half shot of rum; he was willing to ease into this deception a little bit at a time. Leo drank down this second drink with gusto that equaled the first and to the delight of R.E. and the other teammates who watched, the evil plan started to unfold.

Leo continued to work and soon R.E. asked Leo if he would like another. Leo declined but R.E. insisted and suggested that this time Leo try a banana "smoothie." Not wanting to look a gift horse in the mouth, Leo accepted and this time R.E. instructed the bartender to prepare the real thing and Leo was now unknowingly drinking his first real "daiquiri." As the afternoon wore on Leo continued to switch between the strawberry and banana drink until he started to feel peculiar. Leo couldn't figure it out, nor did he know it at the time, but he was well on his way to being drunk for the first time in his life; or at least the first time that any of his teammates were aware of.

As Leo completed his work he commented that his head felt light and the room was spinning. He was certain that it was due to the heat he had been subjected to while repairing the refrigeration system, still unaware that he had been consuming the rum laden drinks. When Leo mentioned that he had better get home to his wife and family R.E. knew it was time to come clean. It was one thing to get Leo drunk, but it would be unthinkable to let Leo drive home in his present condition. When R.E. explained what had happened he thought Leo would explode but to his relief, Leo just smiled and giggled like a child. Several more times Leo insisted that he be allowed to leave for home and each time it took R.E. and several of Leo's teammates to constrain him. Not knowing what else to do, R.E. said that he would call Leo's wife and explain what had happened and ask her to come pick him up. With that, Leo agreed to remain in the bar until she arrived.

I think you can imagine what happened when Leo's wife arrived. She could not find the humor in what had happened that afternoon and for a while it looked like she would take R.E. out back and inflict some real physical pain for what he had done to her husband. Leo managed to quiet her down; after all, the only thing he wanted was to go home.

There were never any major repercussions for what happened that day. Leo didn't change; he would continue his life of health and fitness. As for R.E., he would tell the story of how he was able to get Leo Hamel, the man who never drank alcohol, drunk. And for those of you who think this is somewhat strange behavior, it was and is simply the way of men in the Teams.

41. JOHNSTON ISLAND

A small atoll, Johnston Island sits in the middle of the Pacific Ocean between the Hawaiian Chain and Midway Island. While Johnston Island is only 2.8 square miles in circumference, an even smaller "Sand Island" sits nearby. Both are separated by a small expanse of water. Comprised of coral and sand, nature spent millions of years nurturing these tiny specks. Then one day they caught the eye of the United States Government and sometime later, during the early to mid 1960's, the Air Force spent millions of dollars turning the larger atoll into a military stronghold. When completed, the atoll would serve as a first line of defense against the Russians as the cold war raged. It seems that due to Johnston Island's strategic location, it was ideally situated to serve as an early warning station and defensive military launch platform. In addition, the Island could serve as a missile strike base against Russian targets if deemed necessary.

During this period in time, Holmes and Narver (H&N) conducted dredging activities, removing sand from the surrounding ocean bottom to enlarge Sand Island. When completed, Sand Island would serve as a refuge for military personnel during missile launches or strikes initiated from Johnson Island. This way, if a missile were to blowup on the launch pad, or prematurely fall back to Earth, the personnel assigned to this base would be spared.

Then, during the third quarter of 1964, the Commanding Officer (C.O.) of Underwater Demolition Team-12 received a call from the Air Force C.O. of the military installation on Johnston Island. The Air Force had been assigned to oversee the construction activities related to this project and needed help from the Teams. The enlarging activities of Sand Island had recently been completed, and the Base C.O. asked for two UDT Divers to lay down underwater cable between the two Islands. The cable would provide communications and also support the electrical needs of Sand Island.

Our C.O., Captain Robinson, then called me into his office and said that I would be volunteering for this assignment. Gene Wardrobe, another Teammate, and I were to pack our gear and catch the next plane to Johnston Island. This was a temporary duty assignment that was scheduled to last between two to three weeks, but, in all likelihood, we could wrap it up in one. Before I could blink, we were flying over the Pacific Ocean and would soon arrive at this garden spot in the Pacific.

From the air, Johnston Island looked like nothing more than an airstrip surrounded by a large number of buildings that were under construction. The U.S. Navy had erected the airfield in 1936 and used the Island as a refueling station during World War II. There were a number of older buildings that were being torn down to make way for replacement barracks. In addition, tents lined the beaches and though we didn't know it at the time, one would serve as our new home.

After settling in, we met with an Air Force Officer who explained the extent of our duties. From the briefing, it appeared that we could wrap things up and be out of here in a couple of days; little did we know what lay ahead. Gene and I then went to dinner where we ran across Henry K. "Hank" Lee who had served with us in the Teams. When his enlistment expired, Hank returned to his home and family in Hawaii. He was later hired as a construction worker and flown to Johnston Island where he had worked for the past several months. Hank had the lay of the land, and in short order, we were up to speed on all the places to go and things to see on this tiny atoll. You know that old adage; "Behind every palm tree there's a woman, except there are no palm trees"? This was the case, and it didn't take Hank more than two minutes to explain the facts of life, as they related to Johnston

Island. However, it was great seeing and talking to Hank again.

On the other hand, Hank loved the work on Johnston Island. More importantly, the work on Johnston Island afforded the opportunity for Hank to do what he did best, gamble. The construction paid well and this provided the money needed for the high-stakes poker played here. Hank was in heaven and though this gaming was way out of our league, Gene and I enjoyed watching.

For the next two days, Gene and I worked our butts off, to accomplish all that had been delegated for us to do. We were then told that until the Air Force had plugged in and turned on the power we would be required to stick around. That way, we wouldn't have to be recalled if there was a problem and the cable had to be retrieved. We spent the next two weeks doing nothing. Our tent retained heat, making it unbearable during the day. We swam and worked out and then spent the evenings at the outdoor movie theatre, drinking beer, or going with Hank to one of his poker sessions. All too soon, however, this became a situation we wanted to bring to an end so we could return to Coronado. When asked, the Air Force told us to sit tight and wait, that we wouldn't be there much longer.

Two weeks turned into three and then four and still no indication that the Air Force would set us free. Then one day, a dredging supervisor from H&N approached us with a job offer. He had been dredging a deep-water channel leading to Johnston Island. The channel would make it possible for large U.S. Naval ships to unload equipment required by the Air Force and U.S. Defense Threat Reduction Agency (DTRA). Apparently, the soundings taken in the completed channel indicated that there were three high spots in about thirty feet of water, and they had to be removed.

Gene and I were in our tent when the representative from H&N approached us. His company had decided that it would be much less costly to remove the three high spots with explosives than to go back and dredge the area again. They knew that we were on the Island and that explosives were our main line of business, so they came courting. The representative said his company would be willing to pay for our services, and this immediately caught our attention. Gene Wardrobe then asked, "how much?" A couple of hundred dollars was offered. I said something like "that sounds great," and Gene said, "no, not enough." When asked what a fair price would be, Gene replied, "one hundred dollars for each of us, per shot." My mind was racing, three hundred dollars each for something this simple; I knew he wouldn't go for it. The man took no more than three seconds thinking about it and then said, "O.K. you have a deal." When he left, I looked at Gene, but could hardly speak. Three hundred dollars, unbelievable! For the entire year, the Navy would pay me less than thirty-five hundred dollars and that included double hazardous duty pay of one hundred twenty dollars a month. I was in heaven, but Gene didn't get too excited.

We received permission to do the job from the Air Force C.O. and spent the next day checking out the three areas to be leveled. We then put together a list of the explosives and peripheral equipment we would need from the mainland. In two days, all that we had asked for arrived, allowing Gene and me to prepare the three separate explosive charges that we would place on the high spots and detonate the following morning. Our main concern was to time the shots so that we could light all three fuses before the first shot went off. The distance between each shot was roughly seventy-five to one hundred yards, so it wasn't difficult to figure the time between shots and length of fuse required for each.

The following morning, we went back to the dive area and placed the explosives. A buoy was used to mark each area where the explosives were laid. When we had completed this task, we returned to the first site, then the second, and then the third, each time diving and pulling the fuse lighter. We then sped away from the area in our boat and waited. The first shot went and then a minute later the second, just as planned. Then, when it was time for the third shot to blow, nothing happened. Two and then five minutes passed, but still nothing. We realized that we had a hang fire and set a plan in motion to deal with this problem.

A hang fire can go off at anytime, so it is important to wait long enough and reduce the possibility of the shot going off when you are in the water, directly over the charge, attaching a replacement fuse. Another problem we had to deal with was the feeding frenzy now underway in the two areas we had successfully blown. This was also spilling over into the third area we would be working in. The concussion caused by the explosions had killed a large number of fish, and by now sharks were in the area consuming as much of this free meal as they could manage. In addition, the water was murky from the sand and coral being churned up by the two explosions. This would cause poor visibility, at best.

Gene and I waited for approximately half an hour and then went back to the area of the third shot. I would dive and place the new fuse while Gene remained nearby in the boat, ready to leave as soon as I surfaced. Luckily the buoy was still connected to the third charge, so I had this to guide me. The water was so chalky I couldn't see my hand in front of my face. Sharks and fish were racing thru the water and slamming into me. Then one of the sharks bumped into my facemask, causing the mask to be knocked off and lost in the churning water. I continued swimming to the explosives, attached the new fuse, pulled the fuse lighter, and headed for the surface. Gene pulled me into the boat and then sped away from the area.

Three minutes passed, and the charge blew just as planned. Both Gene and I were relieved, and the representative from H&N was ecstatic. He then told us that he would take additional soundings of the three areas and if the high spots were truly gone, he would bring us our money as he had previously promised.

The next day, as we sat in our tent, the H&N representative came by with our pay. He said that everything had checked out, the soundings had confirmed that the high spots were no longer there, and he was happy to pay us for an outstanding job. When Gene opened the envelope and looked at his check he exploded. The check was for roughly two hundred and forty dollars, not the three hundred we had been promised. The man tried to explain that he had to withhold the Federal Taxes and that this was the standard practice that applied to everyone. Not as far as Gene was concerned, however. Gene agreed to three hundred dollars, and even a dime less than that was unacceptable. When Gene was told that there was little that could be done, he grabbed the man by his shirt collar and lifted him off of the ground, attaching him to a coat hook on one of the tent poles. His shirt ripped, he fell to the ground, and Gene gave him an ultimatum. He could either dig into his pants pocket and make up the difference or dig a hole in the tent floor, where he would then be buried and forgotten. When the H&N representative realized that Gene wasn't kidding, he dug into his pocket and made up the difference. Then, without looking back, he ran as fast as he could from the tent never to be seen by us again.

Another month would pass before we finally contacted our Team Office in Coronado and were ordered home. By now, both Gene and I had reached our limit and were only too happy to be leaving. All together, we had spent better than two months on an assignment that should have lasted no more than a week. We packed our gear, spent the last night partying with Hank, and then flew to Hawaii. We stayed in Hawaii for several days, surfing and having a good time before we returned to Coronado.

Gene and I had both decided to take leave (vacation) upon our return. I would go to Colorado to see my family, but I don't recall what Gene's plans were. We had arranged for this leave, while in Hawaii, so we would simply go into the Team Office, pick-up our leave papers, and take off.

We arrived in San Diego early on a Saturday afternoon and went directly to our Team Compound. What happened next I will never forget, because it was so out of place with the way things usually went down in the Teams. Neither Gene nor I had bothered to have our haircut while we were at Johnston Island. Therefore, our hair was very long; at least according to Navy standards it was very long. The duty officer that Saturday was Mr. Sawyer and when we asked him to sign and date our leave papers, so we could get out of there, he refused. He told us that if we wanted him to sign our leave papers, we must first get a haircut. At first Gene and I thought he was kidding, but we soon found out that he wasn't. Now this may not sound like much, but for Gene and me to go home with hair, the same length as those we were to visit, it meant a lot. This was one of those things you think you can work around, but that wasn't the case; Sawyer firmly held his ground.

Gene and I did get our haircut that afternoon and yes Sawyer did sign off on our leave papers, after we had passed his inspection. I should stop trying to understand why he reacted to us the way that he did; he just did. Until that afternoon, I had relatively few dealings with this man, and I was intent on keeping it that way.

This is a shot similar to one of those set-off at Johnston Island.

42. NAVAL PENTATHLON

This story deals with a very select group of men who served in both UDT and SEAL Teams. These men were not only proficient Team operatives; they were also tremendous athletes. In the early sixties, they brought prominence and recognition to the Teams in a venue not previously exploited by Team members. Their numbers may have been small, but their accomplishments were huge. This is their story.

In 1962, for the first time, the United States sent representatives to compete in the International Council of Military Sports (CISM). This competition would see America's best naval athletes compete against the best naval athletes of other nations. And, while 1962 may not have been a banner year for the United States, with regard to overall CISM accomplishments, 1963 would produce much different results.

CISM is comprised of thirty nations that compete yearly. The program includes events taken from the Olympics as well as specialty events such as the Naval Pentathlon. The CISM general council, at their annual meeting, determines which country will host the event the following year. Athens, Greece, hosted the 1962 event and Stockholm, Sweden, served as host in 1963.

In early June 1963, West Coast athletes began training, under Coach EMC, Don Rose of UDT-11. Chief Rose, SM3, Ron Gauthier, and AN, Frank Watton, all PhibPac Frogmen, had represented the United States, at CISM, in 1962. Chief Rose was, therefore, familiar with the CISM process, a disciplinarian, a gifted athlete, and well qualified to train these men for the 1963 event.

Training for CISM was to be conducted in a limited timeframe and would be very demanding. In less than six weeks, the West Coast finalists would be required to participate in a pre-CISM trial, which would be conducted at Little Creek, Virginia, in July. At this event, ten men from the East Coast would compete against ten men from the West Coast. However, three-quarters of these competitors would leave the event empty handed. The primary purpose of this dual meet was to select the five best athletes to represent the United States during "Sea Week," which was scheduled to begin August 27, in Stockholm, Sweden.

On the West Coast, of the original twenty-seven men selected to engage in the competition, seventeen were Navy PhibPac Frogmen, while the remaining ten came from the fleet. It didn't take long before sixty percent of the original field had been eliminated leaving ten men, including Chief Rose, to make the trip to Little Creek. The final ten consisted of eight men from the Teams and two from the fleet.

Before I go much further, I should tell you that the Naval Pentathlon consists of five events. They include lifesaving, seamanship, a cross-country race, an obstacle course and a utility swim. Each man competes in all five events and his time, in each event, is compared to that of each of the other competitors. Doing well in the swimming events and poorly in the running events, or vice versa, would not send you home a winner; you had to show good and consistent times in all events. I think that you can now see why men from the Teams fared much better than those from the regular Navy. Because of their superb conditioning, proven ability in the water, daily swimming and running, familiarity with the obstacle course, and basic overall strength, the men from the Teams held a consistent edge over most other competitors.

Then, on July 22, 1963, the much anticipated Atlantic Coast versus Pacific Coast competition began at Little Creek, Virginia. As with the West Coast, the ten East Coast finalists came primarily from the ranks of the UDT/SEAL Teams. Therefore, not only would the five finalists be selected from this field of twenty men, but also at stake were "bragging rights" that would go to the Teams to which these finalists belonged. While we were all brothers, there remained strong feelings as to which Coast produced the best Frogmen and this competition, in some small way, would help answer that question.

Going into this competition, the East Coast Team had the home-court advantage, which provided a sizeable edge over their West Coast counterparts. In addition, the West Coast Team had been given only one day to practice on and become familiar with the Little Creek course that had been the training ground for the East Coast Team. Also, the humid weather in Virginia, during the month of July, was nothing like the much cooler Southern California climate that the West Coast competitors had been acclimated to. The only question—could the Pacific Coast athletes make the needed adjustment in time?

It didn't take long to dispel any concerns surrounding the West Coast athletes and their ability to participate. On the morning of July 22, the competition began with a fury but by the end of the first day, the Pacific Team had won both the obstacle course and lifesaving events. On the obstacle course, the Pacific Team placed eight men in the top ten positions. First place went to BT2, Wayne Fowler and second place to SN, Mike Dorfi, both from UDT-12. With regard to lifesaving, LTJG George Worthington, who would later join the Teams, won the event while second place went to SN, Jim Foley also of UDT-12. By the close of the first day of competition, the Pacific Coast Team had taken a demanding early lead, 73 – 137.

The three remaining events would be held on consecutive days. On day three, Chief Don Rose won the seamanship event. Then on Thursday, the forth day of competition, the West Coast Team showed their superiority by taking the first four places of the cross-country run. On Friday, the final day of the event, Jim Foley of UDT-12 won the utility swim, which provided the West Coast with a clean sweep of all events. George Worthington finished first and Mike Dorfi second in the overall point standings. Yes, when all was said and done, the West Coast Team had soundly defeated the East Coast Team 198 – 329. The only thing that remained was to identify the five men who would represent the United States at Stockholm.

With all of the times now computed, five finalists and two alternates had emerged from the twenty competitors. EMC Don Rose, UDT-11: SN Mike Dorfi, UDT-12: SN Jim Foley, UDT-12: LTJG George Worthington, CruDesFlot Seven: and Marine Second Lieutenant L. Gordon Collet, Quantico, Virginia had won the right to represent the United States. In addition, BT2, Wayne Fowler, UDT-12 and Ensign, James P. Wooten, UDT-11 had earned the right to serve as alternates. The field had been identified, and it looked as though the United States would be well represented.

In reality, it takes many years of hard training before men can compete competitively in world competition such as CISM. I didn't include compete successfully in such competition; that takes even longer. The United States would be going up against countries that had competed in CISM for years and, therefore, the U.S. was viewed as a country that came to engage in the learning process, that time consuming process all countries are required to go through. The men from the United States were there to pay their dues and nothing more. Anyway, this is how those other twenty-nine countries viewed it. And besides, the athletes chosen to represent the USA would be competing against the very athletes that represent their respective countries during the Summer Olympics. And, for those men, their primary purpose in life was training to compete in either the Navy Pentathlon or the Summer Olympics, nothing else. Life for those competitors meant training three hundred sixty-five days a year in preparation for this yearly event. On the other hand, the five representatives of the United States had trained for roughly eight weeks in five events that they were seeing for the very first time, so how could they possibly be a factor in these games?

There is one thing the competition had overlooked. They were dealing with a select group of individuals, not ordinary men; most had completed Basic Underwater Demolition SEAL Training (BUDS) and were, therefore, instilled with the desire to win at any cost, and win they would do. When the five events that comprise the Naval Pentathlon had concluded, the United States had done the impossible and finished third overall behind Sweden and Norway. In only its second competition, the United States would walk away with the Bronze Medal. This group of five men had made history. The fledgling United States had bested countries such as Greece, Netherlands, Turkey, Italy, Belgium, France, and Denmark, plus twenty others that had been competing at CISM for years. This was an achievement that had never been accomplished before. And, equally impressive; of the roughly one hundred and fifty athletes to compete, Mike Dorfi, UDT-12, had finished eighth overall. To this day, I marvel at this single most significant accomplishment. For their efforts, the novice athletes who represented the United States had gained the praise, recognition, and respect of every country and from each of the athletes who participated in CISM, 1963.

Three of the individuals from UDT-12, who participated in the 1963 Naval Pentathlon, were my close friends at that time, and they remain my friends to this day. For their above-mentioned accomplishments, they have left a lasting impression, but I remember each of these men for other attributes as well.

Wayne Fowler – on the obstacle course, Wayne was unequalled. That aside, he was an extraordinary self-taught gymnast. Wayne would sit flat on the ground with his legs stretched in front of him and spread wide. He would then put one hand between his legs, push his body about three inches off of the ground, and then go into a handstand and, on one arm, do pushups while his body and legs were parallel to the ground. I was so impressed by the things Wayne could do, that after seeing this for the first time, I immediately went over to a wall and did a handstand; then with my feet against the wall did two-armed pushups. I knew that I could never accomplish the many feats that Wayne was capable of doing, but he inspired me to try.

Jim Foley – Jim was a fantastic swimmer and all around natural athlete. We both graduated from the West Coast BUDS Class-28, in July 1962. We then went together to UDT-12. The thing that impressed me most about Jim wasn't his athleticism but his ability to accept responsibility for his actions and his willingness to give one hundred percent, one hundred percent of the time. What ever Jim did, he did to the best of his ability and no matter what Jim did, when he completed a task, even trivial tasks, he was proud of what he had accomplished.

Mike Dorfi – Mike is a man unto himself. While he was always the life of a party, he was also an exceptional Team Operative, a "Meat Eater," and a person you wanted with you when things got tough. Mike is one of two people that I know capable of doing sit-ups with two fifty pound barbell weights behind his head. If you have a great stomach, have someone hold your feet and try doing sit-ups like that. Mike was also a natural athlete and the only man to repeat at the 1965 Naval Pentathlon. There had been no 1964 CISM because the majority of those countries, who normally participate, sent their athletes to the Summer Olympics. Mike was a friend of mine and a friend to many. I will always be proud to say that Mike is my friend.

In closing, I can only say that I have the deepest respect and admiration for all those men who represented the United States and competed in the 1963 Naval Pentathlon. These men truly defied the odds and define the measure of men who comprise the ranks of UDT/SEAL Teams. With only eight weeks to prepare and train for CISM, they defeated those who had spent a lifetime in preparation. Can you imagine what the results might have been had they spent sixteen weeks in preparation for that competition?

43. LEAVING THE TEAMS

One of the hardest decisions I made, as a young man, was that of leaving the Teams for a civilian job when my enlistment expired. I know that I am not the only man to have had reservations about making this decision, but at the time, I felt it was the right thing to do. The following story is about a ritual, related to making that decision. It is a story about a right of passage that is performed by Team members out of respect for the person that is leaving the Teams, whether that person is retiring or his enlistment has expired.

For all West Coast UDT/SEAL Teams, the Team Compound is located on Coronado Island, an Island due west of downtown San Diego. This Island is one of the most pristine garden spots in Southern California, a choice duty station for military personnel, and the one home I will always fondly remember. The UDT/SEAL Team Compound is located on the Silver Strand, just south of Coronado, and adjacent to the Pacific Ocean. If there is a more beautiful duty station anywhere else in the world, I would truly be surprised. The Silver Strand is an expanse of sand that runs the distance from Coronado to Imperial Beach. It provides a beautiful view of the ocean on one side while the San Diego Bay and Skyline skirt the other. The highway that runs the length of the Strand provides an alternate connection between Coronado and San Diego and provides a more leisurely means of travel for those with extra time on their hands or for anyone not wishing to use the Coronado Bay Bridge.

The Team Compound has grown considerably since the early sixties when there was no diving tower or barracks to house trainees. But of prime importance, the one thing that hasn't changed over the years, is the accessibility Team members have to the water. At the rear of the Team Compound is a large gate that provides access to the Silver Strand

and Pacific Ocean. From this gate, Team members have access to miles of sandy beaches for running, conditioning, and conducting training exercises while the ocean provides unlimited opportunities for swimming, surfing, and training operations.

When Team members have completed a swim, training exercise, or even surfing off of the Strand, each would remove his wet suit, at the gate, and rinse it in a large oversized cauldron filled with fresh water. At one time this cauldron had been used in the base mess hall for cooking soup, boiling potatoes, or any number of cooking chores related to feeding large numbers of military personnel. The point that I want to emphasize here is that the cauldron was very large, large enough to easily hold a man.

The cauldron also served another purpose, one related to this story. On his last day, or the day a man was scheduled to leave the Teams, this cauldron would be filled with water and ice. I don't mean a bag or two of ice, but rather blocks and bags of ice. This would assure that the water was not just cold, but freezing while providing a nice ice surface. Then, the man that was scheduled to leave the Teams would be taken, by force, to the cauldron and dumped into that freezing water. I am sure you can understand why I say he was taken by force, for who would willingly submit to a dunking in freezing water? This is only the beginning however, at this point he would be given a bottle of beer that he must consume while underwater. Not just a part of that bottle, but the entire contents must be consumed underwater or the man is not allowed to leave the cauldron. Also, if he lets any part of the beer escape into the water, then he is given another beer and this continues until he drinks a beer, while submerged.

Now, for those of you who have never tried this, but think it doesn't sound that difficult, I challenge you to accomplish this feat in your backyard swimming pool, without the ice. Make sure a friend you can count on is there to pull you out if something goes wrong. I am really not challenging you to try this; I am simply trying to make a point that while it is difficult to accomplish, this in warm water, it is extremely difficult, if not impossible, to accomplish this in freezing water.

For those of you who think that this is a strange way to show that you care for someone, I can assure you that it isn't strange at all. At least not for the men who comprise the ranks of the Teams, it isn't. The way of the Teams is hard and to say goodbye in any other way would not seem fitting, or at least fitting in the Teams vernacular. And besides, I did say that you were taken by force to the cauldron so that means you didn't necessarily have to be immersed in the freezing water. If you applied all that you had learned in the Teams, you just might be able to fight your way out of this predicament. In fact, I can recall the time a Teammate, Gary Lanphier, fought off six or seven men and won. He was, therefore, spared being immersed in the cauldron.

As I look back on my life in the Teams, I know that I wouldn't trade those times, any of those times, for gold. And though many of the things that happened in the Teams seem surreal, they truly happened then as they are surely happening now. Those were the best of times, and they live as vividly in my mind today as the day, nearly forty years ago, when they actually happened.

For every man who served in the UDT/SEAL Teams, there is one certainty. You may leave the Teams, but the Teams will never leave you. The memories that I have shared with you through the stories written in this book remain as vivid in my mind today as the day they happened. My memories hang primarily on the stories and men who survived the two West Coast BUDS classes that graduated in the year 1962. These men were true warriors and as operators, during the tumultuous years that followed, these young men would be ranked with the very best. And, whether these men remained in the Teams, or left as I did, they carry with them many stories that should be told. It is my hope that some of the men who graduated from the West Coast Classes 28 and 29 will someday tell the stories that only they can tell.

Several months after leaving the Teams and moving my family to Burbank, California, a friend and fellow Teammate, Jay Stansell, arrived at my home late one night. He had made the trip from Coronado to present me with a trophy from the men I had served with. It is a treasure I shall always cherish, not for the trophy itself but rather for the few words that were inscribed on its base; "From the Officers and men, U.D.T.-12, To, R.G. Nickelson, DM-3, "Well Done." These men were then and are now my brothers, and I will forever be proud to say that I was a member of the best combat military organization in the world. I am a proud member of the fraternal order of UDT/SEAL's, may it never change. "HOOYAH!"

TROPHY GIVEN TO NICK NICKELSON UPON LEAVING THE TEAMS. PLAQUE AT BOTTOM OF TROPHY READS:

>FROM THE OFFICERS & MEN
>U.D.T. – 12
>TO
>R. G. NICKELSON, DM-3
>"WELL DONE"

In 1962, President Kennedy ordered the expansion of existing covert and special warfare components of the military. From the ranks of Underwater Demolition Teams (UDT) would come a new unit known as Sea Air Land (SEAL) Teams. At first, the SEAL Teams were comprised of relatively few men and these men were selected based on proven past performance and their commitment to making the Navy a career, sometimes referred to as lifers.

During and after Vietnam, there was a very thin line used to differentiate between UDT and SEAL Teams and their operating capabilities. By the late 1970s and early 1980s, a more even distribution of junior and senior enlisted men populated the Teams and more of these men were committed to making a career of the Navy and the Teams. Then in 1983, because of the similarities of both UDT and Seal Teams, it was ordered that they no longer exist separately but rather be combined. From that day forward, they have simply been known as U.S. Navy SEAL Teams.

From West Coast Class-28, my class, all but one graduate would be assigned to either UDT-ll or UDT-12. The one man selected to go to SEAL Team One was an enlisted man, one of my best friends, and a man I deeply admire even to this day. He was assigned to SEAL Team One, not because he was the best our class had to offer, but rather because he was a career Navy man, a lifer. There were no officers or junior enlisted men selected to go to the SEAL Teams because, at that time, it was unknown if any of these men were committed to making the Teams and Navy their career.

The young man who graduated from Classes 28 through 31 became the "True Team Operators." I can say this with certainty because I knew and operated with these men, I was one of them. And, while these young men may not have been taken into the newly formed SEAL Teams, they were still among the very best operators the Teams had to offer. When men were asked to volunteer for extreme operations, these young men were the first to step forward. When men were asked to test new and previously untested diving equipment, these young men were always first to raise their hands. Yes, some of these young men would make the ultimate sacrifice and give their lives testing the very equipment that is the foundation of today's Navy SEAL Teams. These young men could and did accomplish anything requested of them.